Cracking the HBCU Culture Code ©

Philliph M. Mutisya

& James E. Osler II

TABLE of CONTENTS: *The Chapters in this Text are Provided by Page Number below:*

Library of Congress Cataloging–in–Publication Data

Osler II, James E. & Mutisya, Philliph M.

Cracking The HBCU Culture Code. 1st edition.

ISBN: 978-0-9826748-18-2

1. English Language–Research. 2. Analysis, 3. HBCU, and 4. Culture

Published in the United States.

ISBN: 978-0-9826748-18-2

CHAPTER: 1 *Cracking the HBCU Culture Code* ©

—Cracking the HBCU Culture Code—

Philliph M. Mutisya & James E. Osler II

Conspectus—

Several colleagues and I have been pondering on how to address the climate that exists within and on most HBCU institutions. By and large we have observed how that same climate impacts the overall culture of the institution. Some of us have been in education for some time having served at multicultural and international institutions while others of us have been educated primarily at HBCUs. However, all of us at some point, chose to work at Historically Black Colleges as our main if not final destination. It was not until President Obama was elected that we really started to think on how we could reveal the often *"Hidden"* but actively experienced HBCU unique culture. It is this same culture that effects and permeates our lives on a daily basis, but it is not actively discussed. The Obama administration was the trigger. I am not reticent to say that President Obama's election was the catalyst that sparked the reaction of intellectual curiosity to determine whether or not his election had any effect on revealing the true nature of the American racial climate. This then led to emerging questions regarding racial equity and how much Black Americans and issues regarding Black American life (in all of its myriad facets) have changed or have remained the same.

As a research group we came up with the topic to guide our study of the "Obama Effect" because his election truly set off a variety of emotions by ethnicities other than Black Americans. There were a wide range of responses—some experienced fear; some had mixed emotions coupled with both bewilderment and suspense; others were immersed with hope and optimism; others engaged in a sense of pessimism or outright outrage. Similar to this unexpected change in governmental leadership, we at HBCUs have also experienced various changes and transitions in our respective administrations. The new leadership changes were always met with hopeful expectations. Adjoining the change were new visions, missions, and strategic plans. Yet, there was and is an ironic dichotomy at play. As the hopeful changes took place we also saw many HBCUs diminishing or ceasing to exist. We also faced questions related to: *"Why should they (HBCUs) exist?"* Our observation is not just limited to our HBCU campuses as we as faculty are also a part of the ongoing intellectual discourse that both forms and informs our profession. This manifests as the dissemination of research work at scholarly conferences. By participating and presenting at local, regional, national, and international conferences we were directly involved in addressing the topics that concerned the relevance of HBCUs and the impact that they have on society.

It was not until we came across the book by Samuel R. Chand entitled, *"Cracking Your Church's Culture Code"* when our collective vision became clear on HBCU culture. Thus, we started addressing the cultural climate that exists in HBCUs. It is this culture that tends to be experienced but not openly discussed. It can be characterized as the *"Hidden Curriculum"* according to curriculum development theories (as the *"expressed and emergent hidden learning"*). In this respect we see the HBCU culture as the *"Hidden"* or *"Emergent Culture"*.

Chand (2010) gave us a place to start by providing us with an operational definition of organizational culture and how to decode it using the seven keys. The seven keys are: **(1.) Control**; **(2.) Understanding**; **(3.) Leadership**; **(4.) Trust**; **(5.) Unafraid**; **(6.) Responsive**; **and (7.) Execution.** He also asserts that *"insight"* is the first and crucial step toward *"change"*. Thus, Chand gives us a clear and concise definition to start with as we embark on the sensitive issue of HBCU culture. Another key source that lead us to start addressing HBCU culture was dealing with our own institutional change(s) while undergoing a University-wide systemic restructuring. This pervaded our own working environment in terms of strategic planning in the School of Education where we reside as professors.

Organizational Culture

Chand (2010) defines organizational culture as *"the personality of the church or a nonprofit"* (HBCU culture can be described in this context). He compares organizational culture oddly enough as pornography. He states the latter is hard to define, but, you definitely know it when you see it. HBCU culture meets this criterion. We can actively talk about it, but we cannot define it, and as such, we dare you challenge it. A similar paradoxical aspect of our own ethnic and cultural experience is the existence of a Black Ebonics language. If you ask the simple question of *"Who speaks it?"*—no one shows up. According to Chand (2010) organizational cultures includes tangibles and intangibles. These are the things we can see. Such as the way people dress and behave. The look of corporate offices (such as HBCU buildings and their associated offices). Along with and the messages of the posters that reside on the walls. However, the intangibles may be harder to grasp, but they give a better read on the organization's true personality (Chand, p. 28). He further asserts that the organization's values which whether stated or unstated, its beliefs, and its assumptions; (such as) what and how success is celebrated; exactly when and how the organization solves its problems; (along with) the manifestations of trust and respect at all levels of the organization *are the intangible elements of culture,* which sometimes are identified and most often are camouflaged.

Chand (2010) points out that many leaders confuse culture with vision and strategy which are very different. Vision and strategy focus on products, services, and outcomes. Chand further asserts that culture is about people and it is the most valuable asset in the organization. This raises a very sore spot according to our observation on HBCU culture—especially when Chand points out that, *"the way people are treated, the way they treat their peers, and the way their respond to their leaders is the air people breathe"* **(p. 18).** *As he puts it, if that air is clean and healthy, people thrive and the organization succeeds—but to the extent that it is toxic, then, energy subsides, creativity lags, conflicts multiply, and production declines.* In our 30 plus years of experience in HBCUs we have repetitively witnessed this type of climate. We have observed, less efforts to address the issues but have seen and experienced blame games and the status quo of wait and see who ultimately prevails. In spite of this, however, we must agree with Chand that a strong and vibrant atmosphere stimulates people to be more and to do more. To perform at their very best, reach their goals, and be guided by spiritual leaders who invite meaningful participation, meaningful discourse and dialog from every person at all levels of the organization/institution. We agree that all participants must work together proactively (as opposed to reactively) with a common purpose and a common ideal that is openly discussed and commonly understood. That together we actively share and celebrate each other's accomplishments. In this respect we have observed that within HBCU culture what is celebrated tends to be the *"iconic"* or the *"symbolic"* in nature (predominantly based on a *"We"* versus an *"I"* in terms of culture) and if one does not know the context, (which is rarely openly expressed) but more commonly known, one may mistake it for fake or empty praise.

Question: *"How do you deal with a leader who is reactive and says what you want to hear and when you suggest a conversational idea* (with an aim of making things better), *and the leader responses by saying—"I know that"* (but does not tell you how or what they know) *to apply to the task or the problem at hand?"* It is one thing to have knowledge, yet another to actively apply or communicate that same knowledge in order to shape the attitude you expect to happen or desire to see.

We have openly observed a lack of trust which Chand and others assert is the glue that holds organization together (and gives it the strength to excel). We see that HBCUs accomplish a great deal of ideals which is the reason why they continue to exist. However, repeatedly, we have observed that most accomplishments go unrecognized and thusly, are not recognized which is contrary to the mission and vision of other institutions that follow the same mechanisms and methods of recognizing and rewarding accomplishments as part of their strategic plan and culture. According the Chand the inputs that go into the cultural system includes the stories that surround the staffs' experiences; shared goals and responsibilities (governance); respect and care for people, balance between bold leadership and listening; and clear regular communication. He also points out that the outcomes include the reputation of the leader, the reputation of the organization, and a positive impact on the entire community. We also believe that among the values expressed by Chand, are part of the six pillars of character that make a sound guidelines for a framework for developing a healthy HBCU cultural climate. The six pillars of character include: *"Trust, Respect, Responsibility, Fairness, Caring, and Citizenship"*. these pillars transept culture, region, religions, and all differences. They can be actively used to assess the positive aspects of HBCU culture and serve as a means of truly revealing the *"HBCU Culture Code"*.

Solution: Freire proscribed a process that employs a methodology proven to work effectives on revealing hidden codes of culture which he names as *"Conscientização"* (defined as: *"A Critical Conscious Approach to Dialogue"*) based on the following process:

Naming:

What are the most dehumanizing problems in life?

Should things be as they are? How should they be?

Reflecting:

Why are things this way?

Who is to blame?

What is your role in the situation?

Acting:

What can be done?

What should be done?

What have you done or will you do?

Through the use of "Conscientização" the final analysis should yield and reveal the true —HBCU Culture Code— by empowering the participants to name it and communicate it, thereby accurately defining it to identify with it by at last saying that this is truly HBCU Culture and this is its nature.

Although Chand provides questions that may be used to studying organizations' culture in general, the questions that are useful in contextualizing the uniqueness of HBCU's organization culture (and in the gathering of data that can be used to define the HBCUs' overall cultural climate) for the overall improvement of the institution. The HBCU Culture data analysis questions include the following:

1. *Who are the heroes (experts who make a difference)? What makes them heroes, who determine who the heroes are?*
2. *When someone inquires, "Tell me about your institution" what stories are told?*
3. *How much does the average staff member (faculty) feel he or she has input into the direction and strategy of the institution?*
4. *Who has the ear of the top leaders? How did these people win a hearing with the leaders?*
5. *What are the meaningful rituals? What message do they convey to those in the institutions and outside it?*
6. *Who is rewarded, and for what accomplishments?*
7. *What is the level of loyalty up and down the institutional chart? What factors build loyalty?*
8. *What is the level of creativity and enthusiasm throughout the institution?*
9. *When an objective observer spends an hour watching people interact in the offices, what mood does he or she pick up?*
10. *How the decisions are made, deferred, or delayed?*
11. *Who are the non–positional power brokers, the people who have authority based on the respect they have earned but who do not have authoritative titles?*
12. *Where the control problems and power are struggles most evident?*
13. *How is "turf" defined and protected?*
14. *Is originality in thinking actively supported or appreciated?*
15. *Are alternative opinions appreciated, listened to, given voice or even heard?*
16. *Is punishment the "modus operandi" of those who are or feel that they are in authority?*

Other points to consider related to HBCU Culture:

- A ***"Toxic Culture"*** *is a lot like carbon monoxide poisoning—in that you don't see or smell it, but if you stay in it long enough you will most definitely end up dead...*
- Ultimately: "***Culture Trumps Vision***" (Chand, 2010) — Culture is not vision nor is it strategy—it is instead, the most powerful factor in any institution or any organization.

Other additional contextual resources to be developed further for additional research:

1. Philosophical Cultural Differences by Edwin Nichols; and
2. Intra–cultural, Cross Cultural and Intercultural Perspectives.

Lastly, Comas-Diaz, Koslow & Salett, 1989 state the following related cultural analysis: *1.* Unity of reality and history; *2.* "We" versus "I" worldview; *3.* Preference for call/response; *4.* Strong "in group" tendencies resulting in perceptions of insult when outsiders use "in group" rules without authorization; *5.* Preference for "stylized" vs. "regimented" behavior; *6.* Averting of eyes during speaking direct eye contact during speaking; *7.* Preference for topic-associating discourse strategy; and *8.* Preference for field–dependent (social oriented) learning style; and *9.* Emotional intensity and expression during conversation.

Analyzing Leadership—The Osler Leadership Scale or "[OLS]"

The following Table includes *"The Osler Leadership Scale"*. This Scale can be used to identify types of Leadership. By using this Scale the reader can carefully, circumspectly, and critically observe (as well as analyze) the associated Trichotomous Traits with the type of Leadership they currently serve under. This Scale can also aid in determining the overall culture created by leadership via its defined: Levels, Traits, and Characteristics.

—The Osler Leadership Scale: [OLS]—

OLR Trichotomous Levels	OLS Trichotomous Traits	OLS Titles	OLS Trichotomous Characteristics (That Inadvertently Create Culture)	OLS Numerical Points
Basic OLR →	Trinegative = [–]	*Totalitarian*	Punitive; Instigative; & Toxic	1 to 3
Basic OLR →	Trinegative = [–]	*Overseer*	Oppressive; Pressuring; & Stressful	4 to 6
Intermediate OLR →	Trineutral = [ø]	*Manager*	Maintenance; Unmoving; & Rigid	7 to 9
Advanced OLR →	Tripositive = [+]	*Steward*	Accountable; Solving; & Honest	10 to 12
Advanced OLR →	Tripositive = [+]	*Leader*	Visionary; Inspiring; & Motivational	13 to 15

The Osler Leadership Scale Trichotomous Levels: Key Identifying Leadership and Leadership Culture by Trichotomous Type

OLR Trichotomous Levels	"Are Identical To"	OLS Trichotomous Scale	OLS Related Score	OLS Exact Trichotomous Characteristic Level
Basic →	≡	Punitive Totalitarian → Instigative Totalitarian → Toxic Totalitarian →	— 1 — — 2 — — 3 —	Basic Totalitarian Intermediate Totalitarian Advanced Totalitarian
Basic →	≡	Oppressive Overseer → Pressuring Overseer → Stressful Overseer →	— 4 — — 5 — — 6 —	Basic Overseer Intermediate Overseer Advanced Overseer
Intermediate →	≡	Maintenance Manager → Unmoving Manager → Rigid Manager →	— 7 — — 8 — — 9 —	Basic Manager Intermediate Manager Advanced Manager
Advanced →	≡	Accountable Steward → Solving Steward → Honest Steward →	— 10 — — 11 — — 12 —	Basic Steward Intermediate Steward Advanced Steward
Advanced →	≡	Motivational Leader → Inspiring Leader → Visionary Leader →	— 13 — — 14 — — 15 —	Basic Leader Intermediate Leader Advanced Leader

[Note: "OLR" = Osler Leadership Reading]

Conclusion

All of the aforementioned topics are the ideations that we undertook as we endeavored to *"Crack the HBCU Culture Code".* Our collective early thoughts and discourse laid the foundation for this text. Chand's book was the essential catalyst that provided the framework for an in-depth critical analysis of HBCU Culture. This lead us by proxy to a critical examination of HBCU leadership. *As it is leadership that by and large creates culture.* Our exploration of these topics is not new. In fact, many of the solutions contained within this book are drawn from earlier research that came from the author's early careers. They are presented as chapters in this book. The identified solutions are gleaned from our unique perspectives and respective experiences. These solutions still have applicability. They also have particular relevance and application when it comes to discerning and aiding in cracking the HBCU Culture Code. Additionally, the identified research solutions came about through careful and critical observations of our individual and collective thoughts and ideas regarding our unique experiences related to our own full immersion in HBCU Culture. This led us to begin the accumulation, conglomeration, and formulation of all relevant and applicable career-long topics as solutions that ultimately led to the creation of this book. Undeniably, it is our hope, our calling, and our career-long aspirations to expose the HBCU Culture Code and provide solutions to the *"ambivalent cultural-toxicity and ongoing antipathy"* that currently pervades and plagues HBCU campuses. We aim to remove the toxicity and move towards healing the overall HBCU cultural climate from a pervasively negative atmosphere to a positive culture that enables and encourages all types of growth. Although we critically analyze HBCU Culture we also holistically support the noble and longstanding institutions called *"Historically Black Colleges and Universities".* May this book provide answers aimed at solving the current non-positive culture that exists at these noble American institutions that continue to magnificently serve the public.

References

Chand, S. R. (2010). Cracking your church's culture code: Seven keys to unleashing vision and inspiration (Vol. 54). John Wiley & Sons.

Comas-Diaz, L., Koslow, D., & Salett, E. (1989). Crossing cultures in mental health.

CHAPTER: 2	*Exploding HBCU Culture Pathology Part One: Exposing The Teaching & Learning Classroom Culture*

—The Crisis: Classroom Culture—

Identifying and Analyzing Seven Factors that Disable an Effective Collegiate Teaching Methodology

(Chapter 13 from the Book: A Long Way to Go: Conversations About Race By African American Faculty And Students)

James E. Osler II

Conspectus—

This Chapter as a monograph details from personal experience that young Black faculty encounter in institutions of higher learning particularly HBCUs. Throughout academia teachers, educators, and all manner of instructors have typically encountered "student-based factors" in the classroom that have inhibited the process of learning. The aforementioned factors can be detrimental to the student's ability to progress and are counter-productive to the learning environment as a whole. The purpose of this chapter is to collectively and carefully illustrate seven major student-based factors that the author has encountered that disrupt the collegiate teaching environment and inhibit learning in general. Following the analysis of the "seven factors", classroom management styles will also be discussed to provide a basis of understanding of how channels of communication can break down causing conflict to develop between students and their teachers.

Illustrations and examples of each of the seven factors were gleaned from personal experiences, in–depth observations, and conversations with other University faculty members. Within this chapter the seven factors will be comprehensively identified, critiqued, and analyzed. Classroom management styles will be given the same detailed analysis. The goal is to bring to light behaviors that can cause faculty and students to become tense, negative, antisocial, and embittered. When faculty and students are affected in this manor they create an anti–productive classroom environment that is the antithesis of the process of learning. By disseminating this information it is the hope of the author that a new level of awareness may develop between faculty and students that will allow them to build rapport and remain cognizant of detrimental attitudes and behaviors that can surface in the classroom.

Learning: *The Mutual Human Interactive Interaction Exchange*

The interaction between the teacher and the student is of primary importance in any arena of learning. In the University setting the teacher (i.e. professor) serves, as "the primary conduit of knowledge", and conversely the learner must become "a willing receptacle of content and information". If each person remains true to his or her duties then the learning environment hopefully can evolve into "a mutual learning exchange". However, there is an added level of awareness that the teacher or instructor is responsible for. As "the primary conduit of knowledge" the teacher must always be aware of keeping the flow of content delivery as open as possible. Any obstacle to the exchange between the instructor and the student becomes a barrier to the delivery of content and thus inhibits any possibility of the student's future success.

There is a fine and delicate balance that must be maintained in the learning environment by both sides of the equation. Both instructor and student play vital roles in the learning process. The teacher has many responsibilities in executing and maintaining the vitality of the pedagogy (or andragogy) and the student must be willing and open to learn.

In the collegiate setting there are many required prerequisite skills, skill sets, and behavioral patterns that the instructor and institution expect the student to already possess. These values and knowledge are critical and vital. In addition, the student must become a willing receptacle to the information that the instructor is delivering. A lack of this genuine "openness" is detrimental to the student's success and without "an openness to learn new ideas and knowledge" a student cannot truly excel.

This is the very essence of the process of teaching and learning: content delivery by the instructor and a need to learn to new knowledge and content by the learner. Thus, an analogy of the learning environment as an equation applies; there must exist "a balanced/shared/co–existing level of understanding" between the teacher and the student. Within the classroom an attitude of mutual respect must be established and maintained. By doing so both the teacher and the student carefully focus their efforts on attempting to comprehend, understand, and appreciate one another. In this manner, mutual respect is established and as a result course content, relevant data, and a plethora of information readily flows.

The onus is now placed squarely on the shoulders of the teacher as the primary custodian of the "Realm of Classroom Interaction". The teacher must be at a constant state of readiness and be prepared to mediate any and all situations that can rapidly develop into conflict. He or she must be a consistent "scout" constantly aware of the "red flags or warning signs" that are the signals for a breakdown in communication and interaction.

There are several other areas that a teacher must be aware of to create a trouble–free communicative environment in the classroom. An instructor must be ever vigilant and intuitively cognizant of polluting the learning process and the classroom with their own prejudices and biases. This is an added responsibility by the teacher that includes an ongoing "watchfulness" towards the overall effects of how they go about content delivery and teaching.

As the primary content deliverer, those instructing students must remain keenly aware of the effects and reactions to their method of delivery. The aforementioned are just a few of the great responsibilities that teachers willingly accept when they enter the classroom. Yet, we must not forget that on the opposite pole the student must be dedicated and be able to persevere in their learning of new and different ideas.

Both students and teachers as each side of the "learning exchange" must remain constantly aware of personal wants, needs, and desires that are all inhibitors to the interaction between the teacher and the learner. If unreasonable or left unchecked, the preferred wants, needs, and desires of an entire class or a single individual can detract or obstruct content delivery. Thus, the entire learning environment is endangered. As a result, the process of gaining new knowledge takes a back seat to newly emerged emotions. The conflict now becomes a stifling barrier to communication between the teacher and the student, creating an uncomfortable environment that may become belligerent, hostile, and completely unmanageable.

The Seven Factors That Can Prevent a Student from Learning and Destabilize the Learning Environment

This chapter is concerned with identifying common barriers to the process of learning. A question may emerge as one teaches in the classroom setting and experiences difficulty in the exchange, dialog, and/or communication process with students. The question is this: How can we as teachers (whether we are administrators, educators, professors, or instructors) identify certain key traits or commonly observed behaviors by students that emerge in the classroom and obstruct or prevent the process of learning?

I have experienced and directly observed seven factors that are student–based behaviors that emerge and cause difficulty in the classroom setting. I list them below.

The Seven Factors are as follows:

1.) *Disbelief*
2.) *A Lack of Respect*
3.) *The Question of Age*
4.) *The Need to Constantly Challenge*
5.) *Cultural Tension and Shock*
6.) *Misperceptions of Rigor*
7.) *Lack of Faith*

Disbelief

Disbelief in the instructor or the content is not an uncommon occurrence in any classroom. Disbelief most often manifests itself as silence, awe, and resistance to the instructor and the learning environment. Students may ask questions such as, "You're my instructor?" or "I can't believe you're teaching this course!" Disbelief may disappear once a level of familiarity is established between teachers and students. It is most often annoying, distracting, and an inhibitor to key relationship building that is vital to building a rapport between the instructor and the student.

The best way to diffuse this factor is to address it head on. A student cannot begin the process of learning course material if they are full of questions and not open to the instructor who is delivering the course content. Methods of addressing disbelief include: early and open conversations to create a familiarity between the teacher and student, directly addressing any questions regarding unfamiliarity and confusion, and discourse directly on course content to avoid any and all distractions.

A Lack of Respect

A lack of respect is typically shown or indicated by the mannerisms that students convey in their behavior and actions towards their instructor. There are many ways in which a lack of respect is often manifested. Examples include: abrupt interruptions while a teacher is speaking, conversations during vital course topics or discussions, unscheduled debates or arguments over course–related topics, and students walking out of classrooms for emotional or personal reasons.

The best way to deal with a lack of respect is to address the student privately and directly when the behavior is manifested. If this fails to provide a solution to the issue the teacher may be forced to refer to official class or university policies regarding student attitudes and behavior. The main objective is to maintain class stability, which can be easily disturbed by the random unchecked acts of a single individual. Establishing course ground rules for respect through contacts on set and established classroom policies at the start of the course is an effective way of protecting the integrity of teaching and the classroom environment.

The Question of Age

Age has always been a point of contention between younger and newer faculty and students who are of a similar age or older. Questions on the age of a teacher can lead to a misunderstanding and in some cases be viewed as a direct insult. Often resistance to the instructor because of age can lead to a lack of belief in the instructor's ability to perform the professional duties required in the academic setting.

The most harmless way to address this factor is greatly dependent upon the individual and the set of circumstances in which the question was asked. Some may choose not to address the question directly and may professionally remind students to return to the course subject matter. Others may choose to address the question if the students are not belligerent and are genuinely curious.

The Need to Constantly Challenge

The need to constantly challenge often emerges as a result of the learning environment. This often depends upon the course content that is actually being addressed and student's level of confidence with the aforementioned subject matter. University classrooms are the breeding ground for active discourse and debate. However, the teacher in the collegiate setting must be aware of the difference between a challenging question and an insult directed at their competence and knowledge of the subject matter.

Methods of addressing constant challenges in the classroom can vary depending upon the circumstances. In some cases a private meeting between the instructor and the student may be required to straighten out differences. If the challenges persist, it may become necessary to refer to university policies regarding student behavior in the classroom.

Cultural Tension and Shock

"Cultural Shock" or tension as a result of an adjustment to differing ideals can become a liability rather than an asset in the classroom. This can become an open problem when diversity, gender, and ethnicity emerge as result of the learning environment or become major topics of discussion in the course. Individuals may become angry or confused when forced to come to terms with different points of view from others with different ethnic perceptions, experiences, and backgrounds.

Maintaining the peace and providing the ability for all students to openly express themselves is the key towards providing a viable solution to this particular factor. Class participants must learn to respect the varied viewpoints of others. Keeping a respectful discourse among students becomes the major duty of the instructor. Students must come to the understanding that despite differing viewpoints, experiences, and origins mutual respect is the vital component that they must work at maintaining. If they are successful, they can create a communicative, manageable, and productive diverse learning environment.

Misperceptions of Rigor

Students in the collegiate setting often believe that they are being "hazed" by receiving what they view as "too much work". Rigorous study is the hallmark of collegiate learning. Complaints and complaining by students about workload are a core component of misperceptions of rigor.

This factor is best addressed by referring students to course duties and requirements covered in course syllabi, university catalogs, organizational standards, and requirements for their particular field of study. A reminder to students of their rationale for being in the university setting backed by positive reinforcement may aid in building their confidence. In addition, it may help to suggest that students manage their time wisely and confer with their academic advisor if they are feeling overwhelmed.

Lack of Faith

Fear best describes this factor. Students who are afraid that they cannot meet the challenge of academia fall within this factor. Feelings of being lost and hopelessness are common. The teacher who has a student who is experiencing a lack of faith in the classroom must address it immediately because it can become contagious and contaminate other students who may be vulnerable but not openly expressing their true feelings regarding the course.

Consistency becomes the mainstay when addressing the needs of a student (or students) who are actively dealing with feelings that fall into this factor. Positive reinforcement and strong guidance through academic advisement or counseling may help a student with a lack of faith. Encouragement will go a long way towards building the self-esteem of the student, which is extremely vulnerable when they are experiencing feelings of desperation or despair.

Student-Teacher Conflict with The Classroom Management Style

Classroom management styles can often mean the difference between student success and student failure. How students view their teacher is often determined by how the teacher interacts with students as they deliver their content in the classroom. The following four classroom management styles are those behaviors identified by the author that are typically shown by teachers in their respective classrooms. The descriptions that follow are basic and followed by a brief description of how students may react to the particular style and how conflict and misunderstandings may develop. The following four classroom management styles are:

1.) *The Dictatorial Classroom Management Style*
2.) *The Mentoring Classroom Management Style*
3.) *The Existentialist Classroom Management Style*
4.) *The Apathetic Classroom Management Style*

A Description of the Four Classroom Management Styles

The Dictatorial Management Style

A Dictatorial teacher is unshakeable and firm. This classroom management style prefers to have specific limits and constant control in the classroom. Students immediately learn that this type of teacher operates from a rigid and straightforward methodology. If tasks are assigned then expectations are high that they are completed. This teacher operates from a "no nonsense" communication style. Directness is the key.

Typically one may adopt this style of classroom management when content delivery is at the forefront and time is of the essence. For example, methods courses and classes that require that a multitude of information must be committed to memory in a short amount of time may require this management style. Often the teacher prefers not to be interrupted. Verbal exchange and discussion are not encouraged; communication skills are often not at the center of importance in the classroom.

A teacher adopting this style will want his or her students to display vigorous discipline. Students will often be expected to follow directions and not to challenge or ask why. This may be where the teacher begins to develop a conflict with students. Due to the way that this management style operates students may mistakenly believe that a teacher utilizing this style has little interest or care for their learning or overall well–being. This is dangerous in the classroom because it may lead to students feeling overwhelmed, powerless, angry, and confused. Thus, a teacher with this style must change and adopt the style to incorporate methods for increasing achievement, empowerment, and motivation, through positive reinforcement and encouraging students to set personal achievable goals.

The Mentoring Management Style

A teacher who adopts the Mentoring classroom management style places emphasis on personal growth and development and simultaneously encourages independence. This teacher often explains the reasons behind the rules and decisions. Interaction between the student and teacher are vital to the success of this management style.

A mentoring management style requires a large amount of time. The teacher and the student must interact on a regular basis. A rapport must be built between the two over time. Both teacher and student must be prepared to interact verbally with the student open to regular critique and criticism. The ability to communicate is heightened by the interaction and the student may learn much by watching their teacher perform in his or her duties and interactions.

The key with this management style is the maintenance of a careful interactive balance with the student. The teacher must not become overly dominant, demanding, or intimidating. If this happens then some form of conflict will develop between the teacher and the student. Such conflict may surface as anger, argument, and open resentment.

Positive reinforcement through ongoing praise and encouragement are vital to the growth and development of the mentoring classroom management style and development of the student/teacher relationship. Careful student guidance by the mentoring teacher is the key to success. If guidance with corresponding positive reinforcement is steady and maintained then the student will eventually become self–motivated, self–reliant, and successful.

The Existentialist Management Style

The teacher who uses the existentialist management style places few demands on his or her students. This classroom management style can be best described by the French phrase "laissez–faire" (literally meaning "Let us alone!"). In the classroom a teaching methodology is adopted that is best described as, "Independently Motivated Learning". The learning environment and classroom structure is unhampered and relaxed in its structure. A teacher with this classroom management style allows the student to learn via pursuits that are relevant to student interests.

Difficulty may emerge when the teacher who uses this classroom management style strives be aware of all student feelings and has major difficulty saying no or enforcing classroom policies, procedures, and rules. Further difficulty may occur when there are opportunities for discourse and discussion. Frequent interruption, and a lack of respect towards the teacher and peers may occur if a student with an aggressive personality attempts to assert their values or ideas.

The key towards success with this management style is the placement of a high emphasis on academic concerns and the correct mode behavior in the classroom. The teacher who uses this style must keep his or her students abreast of mutual respect in the classroom. This will protect the class social climate and thereby provide the instructor with the opportunity to encourage self–motivation in the learning environment. This is not always easy and may be extremely difficult when students view their teacher as permissive and the overall classroom climate as easy and free–floating. Additionally, if the teacher chooses to place very few rigorous demands on students, there is a danger that some students who are not intrinsically motivated may have little (if any) desire to achieve academically.

The Apathetic Management Style

The Apathetic classroom management style can best be described as "Focused Independent Learning". A using teacher this style may often be perceived as "indifferent" and is not very involved with their students or actively present in the classroom. Distance and timely engagement via scheduled meetings are traits unique to this form of classroom management. A teacher who uses this style places few demands on the students and appear to be aloof, distant, or generally uninterested. A teacher who adopts this management style wants their students to learn on their own and be totally self–directed in their learning.

An Apathetic teacher does not impose on students. Although the teacher may be present, students are expected to be self–initiating, self–motivated, and eager to learn independently. In addition, teaching by proctor or another agent (i.e., graduate student etc.) is not out of the question with this management style. Constant contact and interaction between teacher and student are not deemed a priority or necessary. As a result of this, teacher and student may not meet until a scheduled appointment time or until relevant course content, assignments, and assessments are due.

Often with this management style students may sense and may openly reflect what they perceive as an attitude of "indifference" on the behalf of their teacher. The danger of this particular classroom management style is that without the teacher as an active agent rewarding students and correcting their mistakes, very little learning may actually occur. An aura of "aloofness" may develop over time. This "aloofness" is dangerous as both teacher and student are vulnerable to this lack of concern. As a result, students may miss valuable opportunities to observe and practice much needed and often required skills. The teacher using this management style may be unwilling or unavailable to offer expertise through guidance and active criticism. If any kind of student/teacher interaction is lacking the student does not receive guidance, learn to meet required demands, and receive ongoing active encouragement. Thus, students are likely to be unsuccessful in their academic pursuits and may decide to give up altogether.

Building an Ongoing and Engaging Rapport with Students and Maintaining Balance in the Classroom

Often a teacher faces a great challenge when attempting to build a rapport with students. Several factors may emerge that provide difficulty in building bridges and channels that can create a positive and dynamic learning environment. Seven factors that can inhibit this process are:

1.) Disbelief
2.) A Lack of Respect
3.) The Question of Age
4.) The Need to Constantly Challenge
5.) Cultural Tension and Shock
6.) Misperceptions of Rigor
7.) Lack of Faith

The challenge may become further difficult if the teacher has not addressed his or her own classroom management style. Four common classroom management styles are:

1.) The Dictatorial Classroom Management Style
2.) The Mentoring Classroom Management Style
3.) The Existentialist Classroom Management Style
4.) The Apathetic Classroom Management Style

Methods for addressing the seven factors and conflicts with classroom management styles involve a committed resolution by the collegiate teacher to become a positive agent of change. Tools such as consistency, positive reinforcement and strong guidance may help a student to become motivated and aid in unleashing their true potential. In addition, encouragement will go a long way towards building the self–esteem of the student and help them to set achievable goals and objectives. Thus, by encountering and adapting to the seven factors and conflicts with their classroom management styles a teacher in the university setting improves his or her students and aids in building a better and more productive learning environment.

References

Osler, J. E. (2004). The Crisis: Classroom Culture, Identifying and Analyzing Seven Factors That Disable An Effective Collegiate Teaching Methodology. A Long Way to Go: Conversations About Race By African American Faculty And Students. Peter Lang. Darrell Cleveland.

CHAPTER: 3	Exploding HBCU Culture Pathology Part Two: Teaching Efficacy Success Strategies

—Teaching Efficacy Success Strategies—
Engaging an Empowering Teaching Philosophy in Higher Education

James E. Osler II

Conspectus—

Defining the Dimensions of Teaching Efficacy

This monograph details Teaching Efficacy Strategies that can be used to empower those that provide instruction in higher education institutions particularly HBCUs. Teaching Efficacy can be broadly defined as a teacher's belief or conviction that their personal interaction in the classroom setting can influence how well students learn. According to educational Researcher Thomas R. Guskey in his article, 'Teaching Efficacy Measurement and Change' (a paper presented at the Annual Meeting of the American Educational Research Association, San Diego, CA, April 13–17, 1998), "Efforts to clarify the definition of teacher efficacy are sometimes clouded by similar or related constructs. It is suggested that the only major difference between perceptions of efficacy and responsibility is in the tense of the items used in the measure, with efficacy representing projected potency and responsibility being an attribute directed toward the past. From the earliest research, teacher efficacy has been considered to have two dimensions, sometimes suggested to be outcome expectations and efficacy expectations."

Teaching Efficacy can be broken down into four major criterions with two primary interacting elements: the teacher and the student. The four criterions are: Preparation, Expectation, Event, and Outcome. These four criterions combined with the two elements may be analyzed in the following model:

James E. Osler II: The Dimensions of Teaching Efficacy ©

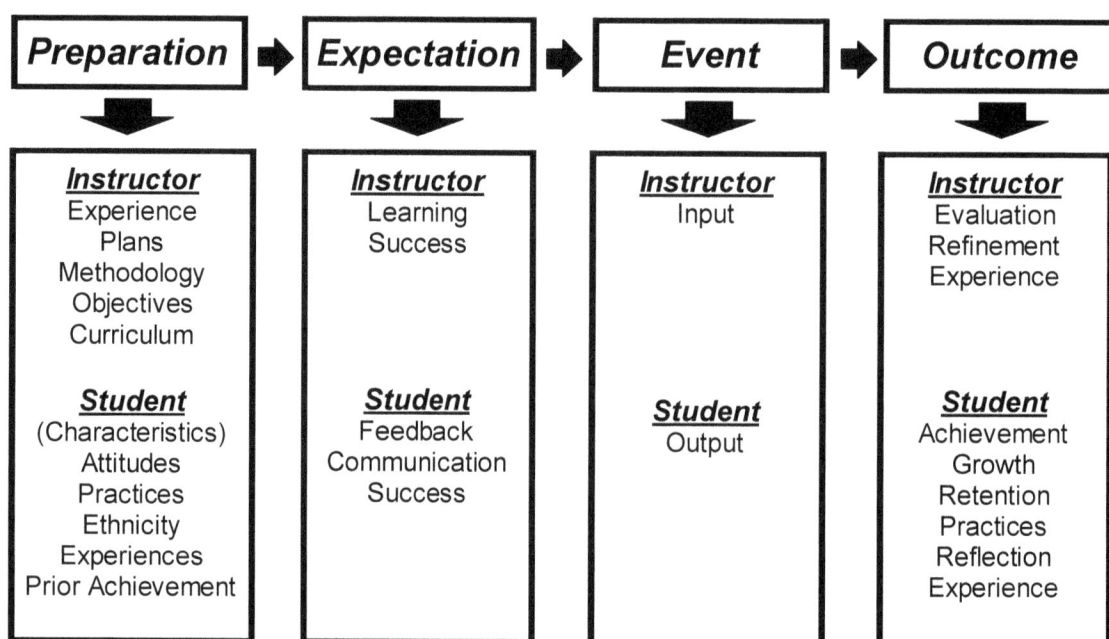

Preparation	Expectation	Event	Outcome
Instructor Experience Plans Methodology Objectives Curriculum	**Instructor** Learning Success	**Instructor** Input	**Instructor** Evaluation Refinement Experience
Student (Characteristics) Attitudes Practices Ethnicity Experiences Prior Achievement	**Student** Feedback Communication Success	**Student** Output	**Student** Achievement Growth Retention Practices Reflection Experience

The model shows the dimensions of teacher/student cognitive expectations in academic setting. Each element (teacher and student) have requirements and beliefs regarding the four criterion: preparation prior to instruction, expectations during instruction, required methods of delivery as the instructional event occurs, and expected outcomes at the termination of the instructional process. There are many strategies and factors that can exhibit successful teaching efficacy. The following section describes how I as a statistics and technology teacher combined my philosophy of education with Asynchronous Learning Network Technology to maximize student learning creating confidence, promote collaboration, and a strong motivation to learn.

The Educational Philosophy of James E. Osler II

Preamble

"All individuals regardless of ethnic origin or beliefs are and should be viewed as equal. Each and every human being is entitled to dignity and respect from their fellow human beings. Each person in American society is entitled to an opportunity to excel, grow, and learn. Thus, each person is entitled to a fair and just education. Those that deliver knowledge (those that we call instructors, educators or teachers) have the responsibility of providing the student with a curriculum that will yield within them growth, development, and a desire to learn. A truly dedicated educator is not only a provider of knowledge but is also a conduit of creativity, innovation, inspiration, and motivation. As such, the educator accepts the very difficult task of trying to inspire within the student a positive outlook towards gaining knowledge and a self–motivated willingness to learn. This in turn will inspire students, empower them, and aid them in their pursuit of the ultimate goal, lifelong learning."

"Education is Discipline and Discipline is Education."

Code of Ethics

Commitment to the Student

1. As a teacher I will attempt at every occasion to provide support, deliver praise, and give as much encouragement as possible.
2. As a teacher I will attempt to inspire each student to explore areas of interest and pursue subjects relevant to their own interests within course subject matter (where applicable).
3. As a teacher I will attempt to expose my students to a variety of interesting and new ideas.
4. As an educator I will strive to deliver to each student current, detailed, and specific knowledge.
5. As an educator I will attempt to present learning in a both challenging and interesting way.
6. As an educator I will attempt to deliver knowledge in ways and methods that increase student comprehension.
7. As a researcher I will stay abreast of new developments in technology and deliver this information to students.
8. As a mentor I will encourage students to pursue their respective goals in education to their completion.
9. As a motivator I will attempt to inspire within students a want to start their own endeavors and encourage them to remain committed to these endeavors to aid in their personal professional development.
10. As an advisor I will try to inspire students to complete research projects in areas that complete their goals and aid in their professional development.

Commitment to the Profession

1. As an educator I will do my best to develop today's students into tomorrow's leaders.
2. As a teacher I will provide my students with very best that I have to offer.

3.   As a professional I will encourage and support any and all areas that are critical to administering and improving education.

Commitment to Teaching

1.   I recognize that I am trusted by the public to prepare students for a highly productive life in society.
2.   The educational system serves the nation and has the responsibility of preparing, tutoring, mentoring, and nurturing the nation's people (elders and youth).
3.   The educational system serves as a training ground for the nation and prepares students to become society's future leaders.
4.   As a teacher I must commit at level to set a high personal standard and become an example to my students.
5.   I recognize that the educational system is the resource from which will replenish our ranks therefore, I must encourage outstanding and exemplary students to consider becoming future educators.

Application of the Educational Philosophy

An Excerpt from the EDGR 5910: Statistical Methodology for the Social and Behavioral Sciences Course Syllabus

Parallel to the School of Education's Conceptual Framework, "Preparing Teachers for Diverse Cultural Contexts", the goal of this course is to serve as a **Mutual Learning Exchange**. In this exchange the instructor will serve as the primary facilitator of knowledge. During this class collaborative efforts are encouraged to promote cooperative learning. Students will use teamwork on assignments and discussions. In addition, students are encouraged to aid and help one another on difficult subject matter and content. The objective is to create an enthusiastic learning environment in which sharing is utilized. This will allow students to synthesize knowledge by taking advantage of their different learning styles, skills, talents, and experiences.

Teaching Methodology:

This course is designed under the principle of "Mastery Learning". Mastery Learning is defined as a group-based, teacher-paced instructional approach, in which students learn by cooperating with their classmates.

Curriculum

Mastery learning does not focus on content, but on the process of mastering it. This type of learning works best with the traditional content-focused curriculum, one based on well-defined learning objectives organized into smaller, sequentially organized units. Students will not progress into another unit until they have demonstrated a mastery of the former unit at a 90% or higher level. If necessary the content of one unit will be repeated until mastery is achieved. This will reinforce content and enhance learning.

Instruction

In this course, the instructor will introduce a variety of statistical techniques. The instructor will also provide frequent and specific feedback by using demonstrations, diagrams, models, formative skill–based assignments, provide positive reinforcement, and regularly correct mistakes students make along their learning path.

The Use of an Asynchronous Learning Network to Develop a Successful, Dynamic, and Interactive Community of Learners in EDGR 5910

Introduction

The advent of computers has greatly changed education. This change has been further enhanced by the development of the internet and vital programming courseware to aid and enhance instruction. Computers and the internet have both allowed educators to broaden their horizons and extend their ability to teach to a broad range of learners that are physically separated from each other and the institution. Many of these learners are at distances to great and widely dispersed to come together as a unified whole in the traditional classroom. The ability to reach these learners via computers and the internet is more commonly referred to as "Distance Education".

Despite the "distance" that is a required and inherent component of Distance Education; the courses that are offered via online networking programs (asynchronous learning networks) can be used in conjunction with interactive and dynamic teaching strategies to create a strong sense of community within the course. Distance Education courses can provide learners with dynamic and extensive tools that allow them to build connections with each other. Examples of these tools are:

- Virtual Chat Rooms
- Discussion Boards
- Electronic Mail and;
- Webpage Development Tools

The use of the aforementioned tools along with strong course design principles that encourage, facilitate, and promote active and ongoing dialogue can create a sense of "togetherness and unity" by the learners taking part in the course. Thus, the instructor can thereby increase the sense of community that is felt amongst the learners by engaging, encouraging, and fully implementing these tools. This was the ultimate goal of the author, an assistant professor in the School of Education at North Carolina Central University.

The task was to create a dynamic community of learners in a Distance Education statistics course EDGR 5910: Statistical Methodology for the Social and Behavioral Sciences (a Distance Education course provided in Summer Session I of Summer School during the 2003 academic year through the University College division of North Carolina Central University). An energetic and dynamic approach was used through the asynchronous learning network called Blackboard/Course Info. (NCCU's Online Distance Education asynchronous learning networks system). The course utilized instructional methods and strategies that took full advantage of Blackboard's Virtual Chat Room, Virtual Classroom, Message Board, Electronic Mail, Webpage Creation Tools, and Posting Options to build a strong sense of unity amongst the learners. The goal of the course was to develop and facilitate the learning of statistics principles and methodologies for graduate studies through the process of discovery learning, teamwork, collaboration, and sharing in the learning environment.

Support for Distance Education

Many institutions are now finding that it is more marketable to reach learners who would not normally have the opportunity to engage in traditional classroom instruction at the University level. There is growing acceptance for the view that educating students beyond the campus is a major element of a University's mission (Harris, 1999). This view is sustained by the enhanced capacity for efficient and widespread use of distance education through advanced electronic delivery systems. Many schools are moving rapidly toward the use of technology to deliver courses and programs at a distance. Distance Education does not simply just refer to computers as the only delivery method of instruction. Several distance education models are presently in use, such as broadcast television, video and audio teleconferencing, and asynchronous learning networks (or ALNs).

Learners use computers and communications technologies in asynchronous learning networks to work with remote learning resources, including online content, as well as instructors, and other learners, but without the requirement to be online at the same time. The most common asynchronous learning network communication tool is the internet through Universal Resource Location (URLs) via Hypertext Topical Protocols (http) for the World Wide Web. The World Wide Web can used in conjunction with e-Learning software such as Blackboard/Course Info. or WebCT. These two asynchronous learning networks can provide University undergraduate and graduate students and their respective instructors with electronic access to course materials, lesson plans, electronic mail, website development tools, grades, activities, and a plethora of communications options such as discussion boards, email, and chat rooms.

Problems that One May Encounter in Developing Distance Education Courses

Distance Education although a great resource for learning is not without its share of problems. One area of concern is that dropout rates tend to be higher in distance education programs than in traditional face-to-face programs. Carr noted that dropout rates are often 10 to 20 percentage points higher in distance education courses than in traditional courses (Carr, 2000). She also reported significant variation among institutions, with some post-secondary schools reporting course-completion rates of more than 80 percent, while others report fewer than 50 percent of distance education students finish their courses. There are a number of well-documented reasons for some dropouts, including the fact that adults sometimes only register for a course in order to obtain knowledge, not credit, and may therefore drop the course once they obtain the knowledge they desire. These are significant factors that must be taken into account when a University is planning to implement a distance Education course.

An additional concern is the actual physical separation of students in programs offered at a distance. This may also contribute to higher dropout rates in Distance Education courses. The separation of students from their peers, instructor, and a traditional classroom can at times be a factor in the loss of a sense of community. Kerka states that Distance Education has a tendency to reduce the sense of community, giving rise to feelings of disconnection (Kerka, 1996). Also feelings of isolation, distraction, and lack of personal attention can manifest (Besser & Donahue, 1996; Twigg, 1997), which could negatively affect student persistence in distance education courses or programs.

The Strengths in Developing an Asynchronous Learning Network Community of Learners

There is an old African saying that states, "It takes a village to raise a child." The same statement may be made in regards to learning via an asynchronous learning network. A dynamic teaching methodology that works in concert along with the functions of an asynchronous learning network can develop a strong community of Distance Education learners. This indeed may be the future of learning that allows educators to greatly broaden the scope and reach of education.

Interest in community and community learning is not limited to the field of education. The last few decades have witnessed an increase in interest in the concept of "community" in general. Much of this interest is based on the perception that sense of community in the United States is weak and there is a need to get American citizens to think about working together toward the common good (Etzioni, 1993). John Goodlad of the University of Washington, head of the Institute for Educational Renewal (1997), echoed these sentiments when he quoted an editorial from the 1990 issue of the Holistic Education. Goodlad (1997) stated:

"Our culture does not nourish that which is best or noblest in the human spirit. It does not cultivate vision, imagination, or aesthetic or spiritual sensitivity. It does not encourage gentleness, generosity, caring, or compassion. Increasingly in the late twentieth century, the economic–technocratic–static worldview has become a monstrous destroyer of what is loving and life-affirming in the human soul." (p. 125)

This point of view is echoed by many modern educators who feel the same about evolving traditional modes of teaching and instruction. Research provides evidence that strong feelings of community may not only increase persistence in courses, but may also increase the flow of information among all learners, availability of support, commitment to group goals, cooperation among members, and satisfaction with group efforts (Bruffee, 1993; Dede, 1996; Wellman, 1999). Additionally, learners benefit from community membership by experiencing a greater sense of well being and by having an agreeable set of individuals to call on for support when needed (Walker, Wasserman & Wellman, 1994; Wellman & Gulia, 1999). Researchers Royal and Rossi suggest that learners' sense of community is related to their engagement in school activities, with students who have a higher sense of community being less likely to experience class cutting behavior or thoughts of dropping out of school and more likely to report feeling bad when unprepared for classes. Additionally, they report that students reporting a high sense of community less often feel burned out at school (Royal and Rossi, 1996).

Tinto supported the findings of Royal and Rossi when he emphasized the importance of community in reducing dropouts when he theorized that students will increase their levels of satisfaction and the likelihood of persisting in a college program if they feel involved and develop relationships with other members of the learning community (Tinto, 1993). This important research can be used to support the building of learning communities via asynchronous learning networks. Thus, empirical research supports the importance of community. Wehlage, Rutter and Smith (1989) found that traditional schools with exemplary dropout–prevention programs devoted considerable attention to overcoming the barriers that prevented students from connecting with the school and to developing a sense of belonging, membership, and engagement. The key finding of their report is that effective schools provide students with a *"supportive community"*. In a study of adult learners in a worksite GED program, researchers Vann and Hinton (1994) found that 84 percent of completers belonged to class cliques, whereas 70 percent of dropouts were socially isolated. A final example, Ashar and Skenes (1993) found in a higher education business program that by creating a social environment that motivated adult learners to persist, social integration had a significant positive effect on retention. The research uncovered that learning needs alone appeared strong enough to attract adults to the program, but not to retain them (Ashar and Skenes, 1993).

Summary

Educators who perceive the value of social bonds in the learning environment must conceptualize and brainstorm how a sense of community can be stimulated in virtual classrooms, particularly in Internet–based asynchronous learning network courses. Learners in these courses are physically separated. However, they can interact with each other through the use of asynchronous learning network tools such as text–based discussion boards, document posting options, website tools, electronic mail, and virtual classrooms (that feature graphical presentation tools and virtual chat rooms). These tools allow learners to interact and communicate with each other without being present and without the requirement of always being online at the same time. Combining asynchronous learning networks with creative course development can create a dynamic and energetic learning network that promotes discovery, creativity, and sharing. These two combined factors are known to enhance the formation of a community, and thereby demonstrate that a sense of community can be created in an asynchronous learning network environment.

Comprehensive Goals & Objectives of the ALN EDGR 5910 Graduate Statistics Project conducted at North Carolina Central University

Rationale for the Project

Courses that are offered via online networking programs (asynchronous learning networks) can be used in conjunction with interactive and dynamic teaching strategies to create a strong sense of community within the course. An asynchronous learning network (ALN) utilizes different tools for computer–mediated communication. It employs the integration of these tools as a means of slowing down the dynamic face–to–face interactions, characteristic of the traditional classrooms, while creating opportunities for the incorporation of a wide range of learning styles (The Association for the Advancement of Computing in Education, 2002).

Distance Education courses that utilize asynchronous learning networks can provide learners with dynamic and extensive tools that allow them to build connections with each other, examples of these tools are:

- *Virtual Chat Rooms;*
- *Discussion Boards;*
- *Electronic Mail and;*
- *Webpage Development Tools*

The ultimate goal of the project was to create a dynamic community of learners in the Distance Education statistics course **EDGR 5910: Statistical Methodology for the Social and Behavioral Sciences** (a Distance Education course provided in Summer Session I of Summer School during the 2003 academic year through the University College division of North Carolina Central University). An energetic and dynamic approach to the subject matter was used combined with the asynchronous learning network called Blackboard/Course Info. (NCCU's Online Distance Education asynchronous learning networks system).

Goals & Objectives

(Objectives that were required to accomplish a set goal are listed and clearly defined after the associated goal.)

1. Develop and Utilize instructional methods and strategies that encouraged:

- *Discovery in the Learning Process;*
- *Teamwork;*
- *An Active Discourse on all Course Related Topics;*
- *A High Locus of Control in the Learning Environment;*
- *Sharing of Discoveries, Methods of Problem–Solving and Resources; and*
- *The Development of a Level of Comprehension that could be manifested in the Final Course Outcome (The Final Project for the course).*

2. Use instructional methods and strategies that encouraged and took full advantage of Blackboard functions that allowed for optimal discourse between the Learners. This included:

- *Ongoing use of The Virtual Chat Room;*
- *Use of The Virtual Classroom features and functions;*
- *Full use of The Discussion Board;*
- *Full use of The Electronic Mail Options; and*
- *Use of The Information Posting Options (for posting Documents, Multimedia, Presentations, Websites, and Other Resources).*

3. The development of a lesson–based curriculum tool (**The Interactive Online Statistics Manual**) that promoted teamwork, unity, and ongoing collaboration through Discovery Learning.

4. The development of a lesson-based multimedia curriculum tool (**The EDGR 5910 Statistics Power Point Presentation**) that aiding in learning concepts and statistical methodology through the asynchronous learning network functions to promote an active engaging discourse; to further develop and promote teamwork, unity, and ongoing collaboration through Discovery Learning.

5. The development of a **Final Comprehensive Project** that was a relevant authentic task that would allow students to fully utilize all that they had learned while matriculating through the course, serve as the basis from which students would continue their learning, and become the seminal outcome from which students could share and implement all that they had learned with each other and the instructor.

The Results of EDGR 5910 Distance Education Course

The goal of the project was to create a dynamic community of learners in the Distance Education statistics course **EDGR 5910: Statistical Methodology for the Social and Behavioral Sciences** (a Distance Education course provided in Summer Session I of Summer School during the 2003 academic year through the University College division of North Carolina Central University). The student outcomes on the final project were outstanding. Sample comments from students included:

"From this class, I learned that numbers can lie, because people who set up numbers could be unethical or have their own agendas. I learned a whole new language, and that Statistics is not as much about math as logic. I think that I think more logically now than I did before, and I will be less trusting of statistics that I hear quoted in newspaper and magazine articles."

"I learned that two heads are better than one. This course was offered an overwhelming amount of information in regards to interpreting data. Statistics is hard, but I learned different approaches to understanding and working through statistical data. I also

learned that information can be biased and populations can be misinterpreted because of misrepresentation populations and also incorrect statistical research."

"I learned that though stats may be hard, if you use all of your resources then its only time consuming. In addition, I learned the best way to analyze research, and the tools I need to conduct that research."

"I've learned that statistics can be taught in a very simple manner so that all can grasp the many steps and formulas needed in order to complete successful research."

"I learned that statistics can be simplified and made practical in its usage."

"Doing stats can be fun and exciting."

"Collaboration helped a lot. I learned that I can do statistics and that it's not all about numbers. It was almost like learning a new language. Thank-you Dr. Osler."

Conclusions and Recommendations

In the final analysis, although time consuming for the instructor the course turned out to be a dynamic turning point in the graduate career for many of the students that were enrolled. In my personal opinion, I find that technological tools can be advantageous resources for the teacher who is unafraid to master them and make use of all that they have to offer. As we continue to grow and develop in education, technology is providing educators with new vistas and landscapes that can make our lives easier and our students more accessible. If we continue to grow, develop, and provide more resources, "The possibilities are endless..."

References

Ashar, H., & Skenes, R. (1993). Can Tinto's student departure model be applied to nontraditional students? Adult Education Quarterly, 43(2), p. 90–100.

Besser, H. & Donahue, S. (1996). Introduction and overview: Perspectives on . . . distance independent education, Journal of the American Society for Information Science, 47(11), p. 801–804.

Bruffee, K. A. (1993). Collaborative learning: Higher education, interdependence, and the authority of knowledge. Baltimore: John Hopkins University Press.

Carr, S. (2000). As distance education comes of age, the challenge is keeping the students. The Chronicle of Higher Education, 46(23), A39–A41.

Dede, C. (1996). The evolution of distance education: Emerging technologies and distributed learning. American Journal of Distance Education, 10(2), p. 4–36.

Etzioni, A. (1993). The spirit of community: Rights, responsibility, and the communitarian agenda. New York: Crown.

Goodlad, J.L. (1997). In praise of education. New York: Teachers College Press.

Harris, D. A. (1999). Online distance education in the United States, IEEE Communications Magazine, 37(3), p. 87–91.

Kerka, S. (1996). Distance learning, the Internet, and the world wide web. ERIC

Osler, J. E. (2004). Dimensions of Teaching and Behavioral Impediments of Teaching Efficacy. Ideas About Teaching Efficacy: Sharing Perspectives. National Social Sciences Press. Gabe Keri.

Royal, M.A., & Rossi, R.J. (1996). Individual–level correlates of sense of community: Findings from workplace and school. Journal of Community Psychology, 24(4), p. 395–416.

Tinto, V. (1993). Leaving college: Rethinking the causes and cures of student attrition. (2nd ed.) Chicago: University of Chicago Press.

Twigg, C.A. (1997). Is technology a silver bullet? Educom Review (March/April), p. 28–29.

Vann, B. A., & Hinton, B. E. (1994). Workplace social networks and their relationship to student retention in on–site GED programs. Human Resource Development.

Walker, J., Wasserman, S., & Wellman, B. (1994). Statistical models for social support networks. in S. Wasserman & J. Galaskiewicz (Eds.), Advances in Social Network Analysis. p. 53–78. Thousand Oaks, CA: Sage.

Wellman, B. (1999). The network community: An introduction to networks in the global village. In Wellman, B. (Ed.) Networks in the Global Village. p. 1–48. Boulder, CO: Westview Press.

Wellman, B. & Gulia, M. (1999). The network basis of social support: A network is more than the sum of its ties. In B. Wellman (Ed.). Networks in the Global Village. p. 83–118. Boulder, CO: Westview Press.

CHAPTER: 4	Exploding HBCU Culture Pathology Part Three: A Culture of Positive External Solutions that Evoke Change

—Technology Engineering Solutions
for Immediate Problems—

(Chapter 9 from the 2008 Book Entitled, "The Aftermath of Hurricane Katrina: Educating Traumatized Children PreK through College")

James E. Osler II, Ed.D.

Conspectus—

The advent of computers has greatly changed education. This change has been further enhanced by the development of the internet and interactive programming courseware that aids and enhances instruction. Computers and the internet have allowed educators to broaden their horizons and extend their ability to reach, train, and teach both colleagues and students. The ability to reach teachers and learners by providing digital educational resources can be vital in aiding those living in regions devastated by natural disasters in re-establishing their learning environments. The goal of this chapter is to provide solutions that have been implemented and are being created for the residents of the United States who are living in the Hurricane Katrina region.

The Problem: The Current State of Education in the Region

As of February 1, 2006 Linda Jacobson of Education Week reported the following: "As students displaced by Hurricanes Katrina and Rita continue returning to their home school districts in Louisiana and Mississippi, tens of thousands remain scattered elsewhere in those states, in nearby states, and across the nation. Five months after schools began rolling out the welcome mat for families fleeing New Orleans and other storm–ravaged communities, officials are still working out graduation requirements, cost reimbursements, and other questions affecting students who can't return home yet, or who are making a new home. According to the most recent data provided to Education Week by state education departments, Louisiana had the highest number of students—105,000—attending schools in the state that are not their home schools" (Jacobson, 2006). Thus, solutions are needed to provide educational opportunities to students and educational resources to teachers who remain in the hurricane ravaged region.

Current Solutions: The U.S. Department of Education's Supporting Americans Affected by Hurricane Katrina

United States Department of Education Secretary Margaret Spellings has stated the following in the initiative on Supporting Americans Affected by Hurricane Katrina by the U.S. Department of Education, "The children affected by Hurricane Katrina need a sense of structure and normalcy. And they need our support. We must not let this tragedy disrupt their education. We will work to help states and communities welcome these students and get them enrolled into schools as quickly as possible." The Initiative to Support Americans Affected by Hurricane Katrina has the following goals and statements:

The U.S. Department of Education Supporting Americans Affected by Hurricane Katrina: Meeting the Needs of Students and Schools

- The U.S. Department of Education is working with states and communities as they welcome the children displaced by Hurricane Katrina and get them enrolled into schools as quickly as possible. In the wake of this tragedy, it is important that we keep our commitment to provide every child with a quality education.
- The Department's Assistant Secretary of Elementary and Secondary Education, Henry Johnson, formerly Mississippi's state superintendent of education, and other Department officials are working in the Gulf Coast region with State and local education officials to determine the full range of student–related and school–related needs.
- The Department of Education launched Hurricane Help for Schools (www.ed.gov/katrina) to serve as a nationwide clearinghouse resource for schools to post their needs and for Americans to help displaced students. More and more matches are made every day between schools needing help and companies, organizations, schools and individuals willing to help across the U.S.

- The Department continues to follow up and coordinate with the more than 50 national education organizations that attended a meeting with Secretary Spellings to determine other ways to coordinate and deploy resources.
- Department employees have joined the effort and are participating in Project Backpack collecting supplies to send to children in affected areas.

The U.S. Department of Education Supporting Americans Affected by Hurricane Katrina: Marshalling Federal Education Resources to Assist Americans Affected by the Hurricane

- The Department is working closely with Congress to marshal federal education resources to best meet the needs of children, families and schools affected by this tragedy.
- The Department provided guidance to colleges and universities to enable them to admit students from impacted institutions in a way that ensures these students continue to receive federal student aid.
- Student loan borrowers living in affected areas will be automatically granted a forbearance of payments for at least three months, and deadlines for a number of the Department's higher education programs have been extended until at least December 1, 2005.
- On a case–specific basis, Secretary Spellings and the Department will be considering accommodations to provisions of the *No Child Left Behind Act* for affected states.

The U.S. Department of Education Supporting Americans Affected by Hurricane Katrina: Good Neighbors — Americans Reaching Out to Help

Communities across the United States are reaching out to those affected by Hurricane Katrina, including:

- In a nationwide effort, numerous states have opened their doors and waived residency requirements for displaced K–12 students.
- Many universities and colleges across the country have agreed to accept students enrolled in Gulf Coast-area universities and to reduce tuition and fees for the fall semester.

Defining Technology Engineering as an Educational Solution to Provide Opportunity and Resources to Students and Teachers in the Region

"Technology Engineering" is both an interactive process and an instruction strategy integrates and seamlessly infuses interactive technology, collaborative methods, and discovery learning with content and curriculum. The author developed this terminology to provide an empowering and effective teaching strategy that takes advantage of the many varied modes of instruction offered by technology in the "Digital Information Age". Technology Engineering is the combination of two distinct yet interrelated concepts combined together as a whole. "Technology" which is the use of the tools and machines that help to solve problems and "Engineering" which is is the application of technology to solve human problems. The two concepts combined create the term "Technology Engineering" which is the product of the two "sets" of knowledge fused together and applied to specifically to instruction (Osler, 2005).

An example of the use of Technology Engineering is the following: Interactive Hypermedia Learning Modules and Asynchronous Learning Networks: Course Management Systems vigorously applied to the course curriculum and is embedded into the structure of the learning environment. These varied modes instruction can be combined with effective Collaborative Learning Strategies to create a dynamic "Cognitive Economy" in the learning environment that delivers the course content in a way that aids the learner in acquiring knowledge (Osler, 2006).

In addition, this new philosophy creates an environment that allows the student to take advantage of their multiple learning styles while delivering a high locus of learner control. Thus, the instructor promotes community and discovery, which in turn, can greatly affect the way in which learners retain content.

Interactivity and Collaboration are required and inherent components of the Technology Engineering Philosophy; the courses that are taught with this philosophy can use online interactive networking programs (Asynchronous Learning Networks or ALNs many of which are now used as Course Management Systems) in conjunction with interactive and dynamic teaching techniques (such as Authentic Tasks, Instructional Design Models, Teambuilding Techniques, Culturally Dynamic Teaching Methods, Collaborative Projects, Learner–Based Tools, Product Based Learning, Hands–On Strategies, and Assignments that include Discovery Learning). This infusion of technology with interactive and dynamic teaching methods creates an enriching experience, innovation in the learning environment, and strong sense of ownership and community within the course by both students and faculty (Osler, 2005).

Technology Engineered course shells can provide both instructors and learners with dynamic and extensive tools that allow them the freedom to build connections, actively collaborate, and express thoughts, ideas, perspectives, views, and opinions (Osler, 2006).

Examples of computer – based tools that foster this type of intellectual academic freedom are:

- *Virtual Chatting;*
- *Video Streaming;*
- *Real Time Interaction;*
- *Virtual Recording and Replay;*
- *Discussion Forums;*
- *Media Broadcasting: News Feeds (RSS) and Internet Radio;*
- *Email;*
- *Teleconferencing;*
- *Voice Over Internet Protocol;*
- *Message Boards;*
- *eJournals;*

- *Graphic User Interfaces;*
- *Webpages;*
- *ePortfolios;*
- *Virtual Development Tools; and*
- *Interactive Learning Environments.*

The use of the aforementioned tools along with course design principles that encourage, facilitate, and promote discovery, positive reinforcement, interactivity, shared experiences, active and ongoing dialogue, and a high locus of control, can create a sense of togetherness and empowerment by both faculty and students enrolled in the course. Thus, the instructor can thereby increase interest in the subject matter, encourage learning, and continue to develop a global sense of ownership that is both empowering and innovative. This is the ultimate goal of Technology Engineering.

The Foundations of Technology Engineering

Previous work by the author involved the development of effective Interactive Ergonomic Learner – Based Tools and their seamless infusion into course content. Inquiry in this arena led interesting questions such as: "Is it possible to combine subject matter and interactive tools to increase subject matter retention and transfer?" Results of this research went well past the initial expectations. Added outcomes included comments that were lively, engaging, enjoyable and unexpectedly empowering for both students and faculty. Further study and attempts to rationalize, add meaning, and a more global structure to the process yielded a new terminology for this particular method of instruction. Results of this new method of instruction determined that it had an unexpectedly powerful outcome.

The outcome of the new methodology was the development of a dynamic empowering learning community that could only be termed an "Interactive Cognitive Economy" (an "Interactive Cognitive Economy" takes advantage of the unity of collaboration, with meaningful relevance to subject matter and content, the delivery of challenging and engaging learning activities, though the lens of relevant and meaningful performance objectives and goals). In a "technologically engineered interactive cognitive economy" faculty and students become active learners who are consciously engaged in building, developing, creating, changing, challenging, and advocating. By combining experiences and viewpoints with instructional design, technology, interactivity, discovery, relevance, collaboration, creativity, and innovation new heights were in academics and self – awareness. The new instructional methodology was titled: "Technology Engineering".

The courses that were "Technologically Engineered" were EDU 3700: Statistical Methodology for the Social and Behavioral Sciences (undergraduate) EDGR 5910: Statistical Methodology for the Social and Behavioral Sciences (graduate). The courses were taught in three different methods over a period of two years (2003 to 2005) traditionally, at a distance, and web–enhanced. Courses were provided by both the School of Education (traditional and web–enhanced) and the University College (distance education) of North Carolina Central University. The courses utilized instructional methods and strategies that took full advantage of the Internet Resources, Virtual Chatting, Virtual Assessments, Competence

Mastery Tests, Interactive Media, Virtual Classrooms, Electronic Mail, and Discussion Forums to build a strong sense of unity amongst the learners. The goal of the courses (both graduate and undergraduate) was to make the Statistics course content meaningful, relevant, engaging and empowering.

Technology Engineering Develops an Effective Ergonomic Learner–Centered Approach to Teaching: "A Dynamic Interactive Cognitive Economy"

Teaching can best be described as "The Profession of Empowering". It is often underrated, unheralded, and unappreciated. It is a process of constant extremes. It can be simultaneously frustrating and joyous or dramatic and foreboding. At every level, virtually all teachers agree that the process of teaching can be at times both difficult and rewarding.

Teachers face constant challenges. Yet, with a nurturing and pioneering spirit a teacher can become an interactive agent in a lifelong career of empowering others. It is at this ultimate height that the profession of teaching boasts of workers who are tremendously dedicated and intrinsically motivated. These qualities are so much a part of the profession that despite the many challenges (and many times against the greatest of odds) teachers often succeed and produce astounding results (Osler, 2006).

In terms of curriculum, many of the difficulties that teachers often encounter can be typically found in two major areas. The first area of concern is the transfer of content to the learner and the second area of concern is the student's ability to perform (at a required or specified level) with the new knowledge. Further difficulty can develop when the instructor requires the student to think critically and/or apply content and knowledge to a given situation (thus demonstrating the ability to synthesize and expound upon data).

There are a plethora of teaching strategies and methodologies that may be applied and utilized in any instructional setting. Many of these strategies are concerned with the methodologies of how information is disseminated, delivered, and processed. In many cases, an instructor may devise their own unique strategies to meet the demands of a given learning environment or situation when no other strategies or methodologies are available.

Some teaching methods place an emphasis on rote lecture; others may emphasize learning styles, performance criteria or a systematic approach. It is this author's hope that through a "Technology Engineering" methodology that involves the effective combination of technology (such as Interactive Hypermedia Learning Modules [Interactive Hypermedia and Interactive Graphic User Interfaces], Online Tools [Websites, WebQuests, Blogs, and RSS feeds] and Asynchronous Learning Networks [Course Shells, ePortfolio data storage systems, and data management networks]) educators will have access to a plethora of resources that will aid them in developing effective learning environments. Hopefully, through the use of effective Technology Engineering the art of teaching will become efficient, effective, and empowering to both the teacher and the learner (Osler, 2006).

Technology Engineering Elements

Many institutions are now finding that it is more marketable to reach learners who would not normally have the opportunity to engage in traditional classroom instruction at the University level. There is growing acceptance for the view that educating students beyond the campus is a major element of a University's mission (Harris, 1999). This view is sustained by the enhanced capacity for efficient and widespread use of distance education through advanced electronic delivery systems. Many schools are moving rapidly toward the use of technology to deliver courses and programs at a distance. Distance Education does not simply just refer to computers as the only delivery method of instruction. Several distance education models are presently in use, such as broadcast television, video and audio teleconferencing, and Asynchronous Learning Networks.

Learners use computers and communications technologies in asynchronous learning networks to work with remote learning resources, including online content, as well as instructors, and other learners, but without the requirement to be online at the same time. The most common asynchronous learning network communication tool is the internet through Universal Resource Location (URLs) via Hypertext Topical Protocols (http) for the World Wide Web. The World Wide Web can used in conjunction with e–Learning software such as Blackboard or WebCT. These two asynchronous learning networks can provide University undergraduate and graduate students and their respective instructors with electronic access to course materials, lesson plans, electronic mail, website development tools, grades, activities, and a plethora of communications options such as discussion boards, email, and chat rooms.

The Rational for the Online Technology Engineering Solution

Distance Education although a great resource for learning is not without its share of problems. One area of concern is that dropout rates tend to be higher in distance education programs than in traditional face–to–face programs. Carr noted that dropout rates are often 10 to 20 percentage points higher in distance education courses than in traditional courses (Carr, 2000). She also reported significant variation among institutions, with some post–secondary schools reporting course–completion rates of more than 80 percent, while others report fewer than 50 percent of distance education students finish their courses. There are a number of well–documented reasons for some dropouts, including the fact that adults sometimes only register for a course in order to obtain knowledge, not credit, and may therefore drop the course once they obtain the knowledge they desire. These are significant factors that must be taken into account when a University is planning to implement a distance Education course.

An additional concern is the actual physical separation of students in programs offered at a distance. This may also contribute to higher dropout rates in Distance Education courses. The separation of students from their peers, instructor, and a traditional classroom can at times be a factor in the loss of a sense of community. Kerka states that Distance Education has a tendency to reduce the sense of community, giving rise to feelings of disconnection (Kerka, 1996). Also feelings of isolation, distraction, and lack of personal attention can manifest (Besser & Donahue, 1996; Twigg, 1997), which could negatively affect student persistence in distance education courses or programs.

The Technology Engineering Solutions for the Hurricane Katrina Region: A Face to Face Interactive Lab Conducted in the Region by InspireWorks © and an Online Information Network in the School of Education at North Carolina Central University

This Chapter will provide two technology solutions that exemplify outstanding Technology Engineering. These solutions have and can provide aid education in the Hurricane Katrina region. The face to face solution was been implemented and occurred in Shreveport, Louisiana with the Praise Temple Full Gospel Baptist Church by InspireWorks © and was called InspireCamp ©. The online solution is currently being developed as an online resource on the content management system (an Asynchronous Learning Network or "ALN" called Blackboard 7.0) in the School of Education at North Carolina Central University.

The Face to Face Technology Engineering Solution: InspireCamp © by InspireWorks ©

Figure One. The InspireWorks © Headquarters:

InpsireWorks © was a software development and technology company based in Florham Park, New Jersey and Cary, North Carolina (see Figure One). Jim Tagliareni founded InspireWorks ©, in May 2002, and his vision and mission were to move beyond the traditional data tools and processes that were prevalent in industry at that time. Mr. Tagliareni assembled a dynamic development team that had many years of experience in delivering infrastructure platforms and applications for computer systems.

The InspireWorks © team at the time in which the Hurricane Katrina disaster occurred had built a code base for an on-demand horizontal computerized system that served several vertical markets: Education, Sports, Entertainment, Advertising, and the Corporate arena. One area of this horizontal system (which was specifically designed for the education market), is called InspireCamp ©, a digital day camp that had been running across the country.

Figure Two. The InspireCamp © Structure:

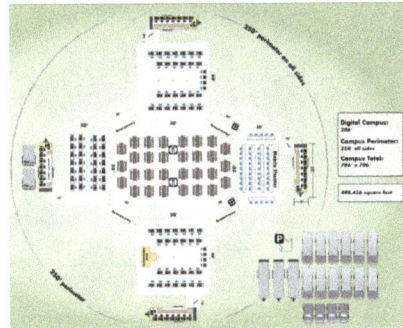

InspireWorks © enjoyed the summer of 2005 providing digital day camps in the state of New Jersey and partnering with a program sponsored by the New Jersey State Attorney General's Office, called "Project Vision – Adventure Club". "Project Vision – Adventure Club" were technology–based camps for children. These camps allowed children to create digital film projects reflecting life experiences.

Figure Three. The InspireCamp © Interior:

When the Hurricane Katrina Disaster took place InspireWorks © decided to offer help to the gulf coast residents affected by Hurricane Katrina. Jim Tagliareni decided that InspireWorks © would go to the gulf coast region and set up a fun after–school digital day camp for school children ranging in ages 5 to 18 (or K – 12th grade). The technology camp was set up in Shreveport, Louisiana as an collaborative effort with the Praise Temple Full Gospel Baptist Church. Praise Temple made available over 2 acres of land to establish the digital campus. The camp was operated by InspireWorks' employees and volunteers. The camp facilities were made up of 150 computer workstations, four 50–foot tents with breezeways, 3 mobile video production studios, and an eating area designed to seat up to 300 individuals (see Figure Two).

Figure Four. The InspireCamp © in Action:

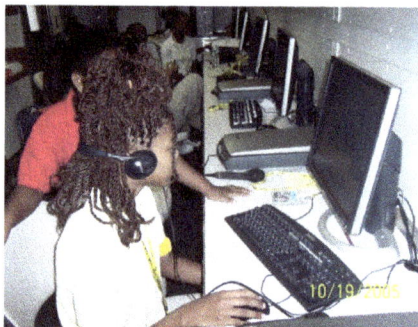

The camp curriculum was set up with 10 interactive modules (see Figure Three). Topics ranged from Introduction to the Digital Production Process, Script Writing, DVD Authoring, I AM, to specialty courses, such as Earth Science. The children partnered in groups to create personal DVDs, each with constructivist hands–on time on the computer. The goal of the Shreveport camp was to provide a diversion from the recent events brought on by Hurricane Katrina and to give the children a different outlet; knowledge of the digital process, and a way to deal with life's challenges by re–emphasizing the importance of education. In addition, the camp included remedial tutorials in mathematics and language arts. A special time set aside for the students to complete their assignments and homework, specialized sessions took place on life skills and ethical sessions were conducted that placed emphasis on good morals (see Figure Four).

Several keynote speakers were invited and motivated and encouraged the campers as well as the community. Invited speakers included: Senate Chaplain Barry Black, Dr. Wintley Phipps, Bishop Paul S. Morton, and Bishop W. Todd Ervin. Each offered rousing, power–packed, and encouraging messages. On Friday of each week, the camp finale was conducted and concluded with the presentation of the personal DVDs created by the children which were shown to their parents, friends, community and citywide leaders. The InspireCamp © was a success and greatly aided in the residents in the region in enhancing their quality of life.

The Online Technology Engineering Solution: The Hurricane Katrina Online Educational Network © a Resource for Teachers

Figure Five. The Hurricane Katrina Online Educational Network ©:

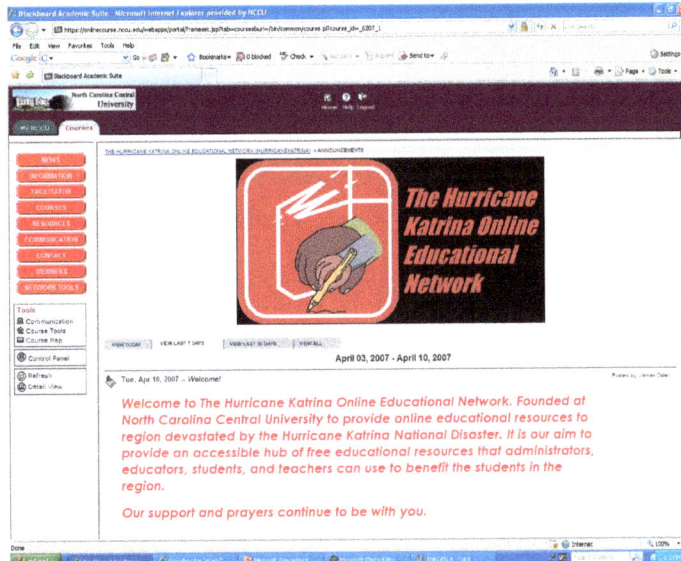

Educators who perceive the value of social bonds in the learning environment can envision and conceptualize how a sense of community can be stimulated in virtual classrooms, particularly in Internet–based asynchronous learning network courses and content management systems. The purpose of The Hurricane Katrina Online Educational Network © is to provide an online digital Resource for Teachers in the hurricane Katrina region (see Figure Five).

Through this newly created centralized educational online resource teachers in the Hurricane affected region will soon be able to interact with peers and colleagues throughout the country through the use of asynchronous learning network tools such as text–based discussion boards, document posting options, website tools, electronic mail, and virtual classrooms (that feature graphical presentation tools and virtual chat rooms). These tools allow teachers to interact and communicate with each other without being present and without the requirement of always being online at the same time. Combining asynchronous learning networks with creative course development resources can create a dynamic and energetic learning network that promotes discovery, creativity, and sharing. The aforementioned factors are known to enhance the formation of a community, and thereby demonstrate that a sense of community can be created in an asynchronous learning network environment.

There is an old African saying that states, "*It takes a village to raise a child.*" The same statement may be made in regards to the provision of teaching resources and aid via asynchronous learning network/course management systems. A dynamic teaching methodology that works in concert along with the functions of an asynchronous learning network can develop a strong community of teachers and provide them with rapidly with much needed resources. This in turn, allows educators to greatly broaden the scope and reach of education.

Interest in community and community learning is not limited to the field of education. The last few decades have witnessed an increase in interest in the concept of "community" in general. Much of this interest is based on the perception that sense of community in the United States is weak and there is a need to get American citizens to think about working together toward the common good (Etzioni, 1993). John Goodlad of the University of Washington, head of the Institute for Educational Renewal (1997), echoed these sentiments when he quoted an editorial from the 1990 issue of the Holistic Education. Goodlad (1997) stated:

"Our culture does not nourish that which is best or noblest in the human spirit. It does not cultivate vision, imagination, or aesthetic or spiritual sensitivity. It does not encourage gentleness, generosity, caring, or compassion. Increasingly in the late twentieth century, the economic–technocratic–static worldview has become a monstrous destroyer of what is loving and life-affirming in the human soul." (p. 125)

This point of view is echoed by many modern educators who feel the same about evolving traditional modes of teaching and instruction. Research provides evidence that strong feelings of community may not only increase persistence in courses, but may also increase the flow of information among all learners, availability of support, commitment to group goals, cooperation among members, and satisfaction with group efforts (Bruffee, 1993; Dede, 1996; Wellman, 1999). Additionally, learners benefit from community membership by experiencing a greater sense of well being and by having an agreeable set of individuals to call on for support when needed (Walker, Wasserman & Wellman, 1994; Wellman & Gulia, 1999). Researchers Royal and Rossi suggest that learners' sense of community is related to their engagement in school activities, with students who have a higher sense of community being less likely to experience class cutting behavior or thoughts of dropping out of school and more likely to report feeling bad when unprepared for classes. Additionally, they report that students reporting a high sense of community less often feel burned out at school (Royal and Rossi, 1996).

Tinto supported the findings of Royal and Rossi when he emphasized the importance of community in reducing dropouts when he theorized that students will increase their levels of satisfaction and the likelihood of persisting in a college program if they feel involved and develop relationships with other members of the learning community (Tinto, 1993). This important research can be used to support the building of learning communities via asynchronous learning networks. Thus, empirical research supports the importance of community. Wehlage, Rutter and Smith (1989) found that traditional schools with exemplary dropout–prevention programs devoted considerable attention to overcoming the barriers that prevented students from connecting with the school and to developing a sense of belonging, membership, and engagement. The key finding of their report is that effective schools provide students with a "supportive community". In a study of adult learners in a worksite GED program, researchers Vann and Hinton (1994) found that 84 percent of completers belonged to class cliques, whereas 70 percent of dropouts were socially isolated.

A final example, Ashar and Skenes (1993) found in a higher education business program that by creating a social environment that motivated adult learners to persist, social integration had a significant positive effect on retention. The research uncovered that learning needs alone appeared strong enough to attract adults to the program, but not to retain them (Ashar and Skenes, 1993).

Courses and resources that are offered via online networking programs (Asynchronous Learning Networks/Course management Systems) can be used in conjunction with interactive and dynamic teaching strategies to create a strong sense of community. This model may be very advantageous to the Hurricane Katrina and Rita regions were non-traditional means of resources may be the answer to a lack of infrastructure that greatly affects the learning environment. Currently, the Massachusetts Institute of Technology (MIT) has a $100.00 Laptop initiative that uses the internet to provide content. This initiative in conjunction with the use of the Technology Engineered solutions such as InspireWorks © InspireCamp ©, The Hurricane Katrina Online Educational Network © could rebuild the learning environment in the hurricane region in a proactive, positive, and progressive way.

Conclusion

Technology Engineering is an empowering philosophy, practice, and methodology that combines resources and computing with an interactive and dynamic instructional strategies. It can be used empower both students and teachers in the Hurricane Katrina region who can readily take advantage of the resources to improve their lives and rebuild their learning environment. As we continue to grow and develop in education, the proper use and implementation of innovative and interactive technology is providing educators with new territory to explore and new resources to share.

Sharing of time and resources can prove to be invaluable to those affected by natural disasters. In many cases it can literally make a difference with those who are suffering from extreme loss. As we explore and share in this new arena of Technology Engineering we make the art of teaching more effective, more valuable, more dynamic, and more accessible. The results can be rather dramatic. Students who may have once been intimidated by the course content and teachers who may have once lacked vital resources; can transform into pioneering giants. They may now bristle with confidence, when they were once broken by traumatic experiences. Effective Technology Engineering at its very core is an art that is composed of just the right combination of: curriculum, creativity, technology, and the profound desire to share through love.

In the "Information Age" we are boundless and as limitless as our imagination. New pedagogical and andragogical methods are being developed by those who interact and teach students with technological tools. Technology Engineering has the ability to transform individuals, environments, and institutions. The end results may prove to be as far reaching as the early printing press and have the unlimited potential to take the art of teaching to previously unforeseen heights. Thus, our future is bright and the positive implications are limitless.

References

Ashar, H. and Skenes, R., 1993. Can Tinto's Student Departure Model be Applied to Nontraditional Students? *Adult Education Quarterly*, Vol. 43, No. 2, pp. 90–100.

Besser, H. and Donahue, S., 1996. Introduction and Overview: Perspectives on Distance Independent Education, *Journal of the American Society for Information Science*, Vol. 47, No. 11, pp. 801–804.

Bruffee, K. A., 1993. *Collaborative Learning: Higher Education, Interdependence, and the Authority of Knowledge.* John Hopkins University Press, Baltimore, USA.

Carr, S., 2000. As Distance Education Comes of Age, the Challenge is Keeping the Students. *The Chronicle of Higher Education*, Vol. 46, No. 23, pp. A39–A41.

Dede, C., 1996. The Evolution of Distance Education: Emerging Technologies and Distributed Learning. *American Journal of Distance Education*, Vol. 10, No. 2, pp. 4–36.

Downing, D. (1987). Dictionary of Mathematical Terms. Hauppauge, NY: Barron's Educational Series, Inc.

Etzioni, A., 1993. *The Spirit of Community: Rights, Responsibility, and the Communitarian Agenda.* Crown, New York, USA.

Galaskiewicz J. and Wasserman S., 1994. Advances in Social Network Analysis. *SAGE Focus Editions.* Vol. 171, pp. 53–78.

Goodlad, J. L., 1997. *In Praise of Education.* Teachers College Press, New York, USA.

Harris, D. A., 1999. Online Distance Education in the United States, *IEEE Communications Magazine*, Vol. 37, No. 3, pp. 87–91.

Jacobson, L., 2006. Hurricanes' aftermath is ongoing. *Education Week.* Vol. 25, No. 21, 1–18.

Kerka, S., 1996. *Distance learning, the Internet, and the World Wide Web.* Education Resources Information Center, Lanham, USA.

Osler, J. E. (2005). *Technology Engineering: Developing, implementing, and infusing interactive hypermedia learning modules into an asynchronous learning network to develop an interactive community of learners.* Interactive Presentation and Paper Presented at The 2005 South Atlantic Philosophy of Education Society Refereed Annual Yearbook.

Osler, J. E. (2006). *Technology Engineering: a paradigm shift to promote academic freedom in the information age.* The South Atlantic Philosophy of Education Society Refereed Annual Yearbook.

Osler, J. E. (2008). *Chapter 9: Technology Engineering Educational Solutions for the Hurricane Katrina Region. The Aftermath of Hurricane Katrina: Educating Traumatized Children PreK through College.* University Press of America. Edited by Dorothy Singleton. pp. 104–120.

Royal, M.A. and Rossi, R.J., 1996. Individual-Level Correlates of Sense of Community: Findings from Workplace and School. *Journal of Community Psychology*, Vol. 24, No. 4, pp. 395–416.

Tinto, V., 1993. *Leaving college: Rethinking the causes and cures of student attrition.* University of Chicago Press., Chicago, USA.

Twigg, C.A., 1997. Is Technology a Silver Bullet? *Educom Review*, Vol. 31, No. 2, pp. 28–29.

Vann, B. A. et al, 1994. Workplace Social Networks and Their Relationship to Student Retention in On-Site GED Programs. *Human Resource Development Quarterly*, Vol.. 5, No. 2, pp. 141–51.

United States Department of Education (2006). *Supporting Americans affected by hurricane Katrina.* www.ed.gov/katrina.

Walker, J. et al, 1994. Statistical Models for Social Support Networks. *SAGE Focus Editions.* Vol. 171, pp. 40–53.

Wellman, B., 1999. *Networks in the Global Village.* Westview Press, Boulder, USA.

Wellman, B., 1999. *Networks in the Global Village: The Network Community: An Introduction to Networks in the Global Village.* Westview Press, Boulder, USA.

Wellman, B. and Gulia, M., 1999. *Networks in the Global Village: The Network Basis of Social Support: A Network is More than the Sum of its Ties.* Westview Press, Boulder, USA.

| C<small>HAPTER:</small> 5 | *Exploding HBCU Culture Pathology Part Four: Self–Actualization through Self–Discovery* |

—The Road to Self–Discovery—
Finding One's True Self is the First Step Towards Completing One's Divine Calling

James E. Osler II

"Therefore being justified by faith, we have peace with GOD."

Romans 5: 1

Conspectus—

In ancient Kemet or Africa, institutions of higher learning had a solitary motto that set the tone for learning and the overall mission for various forms of study. This motto or creed was simply, "Know Thyself". It was through this theme that the student came to realize that the entire process of learning and study was simply a process of gaining self–actualization and thereby creating a movement towards "Universal Understanding".

The "Know Thyself" theme was an ever–present reminder that life is a constant process of self–discovery. It is through this "process", which can be actively termed as "life–long learning" that we enter into many different endeavors and experience many meaningful events. It is only through our own determination, talent, and persistence that we complete the varying tasks, goals, and objectives that will allow each of us to ultimately discover and define our purpose and define our true self.

The journey of "self–discovery" is the journey in life that defines, broadens, and allows us to similarly relate to other human beings who are walking a similar path. Those who embrace the arduous path of "self knowledge" or "self–discovery" ultimately come into contact with "Universal Love" and are often regarded as loving or "truly spiritual beings". The goal of the spirit or those who are in essence "living spiritual beings" is to raise their consciousness to a level of awareness that is universal and expressed through "Universal Love".

In essence, a person seeks to essentially come into greater contact with their creator. By doing so they thereby become one with the universe, all of life, and all beings. This state of awareness is transcendental and is often referred to in many religions as "True Enlightenment".

How enlightenment is defined can vary from individual to individual due to religious beliefs, nationality, or personal preference. True "Enlightenment" is a broad term that can be defined by a large number of definitions. However, most spiritual scholars will agree that "True Inner Enlightenment" is an ongoing internal process that involves sharing, caring, giving, and completely understanding love. How one chooses to "love" or express "love" can greatly vary and is deeply personal. This "process of expressing love" has relevance to, and can only be defined by, an individual.

We may then ask a question. "How does one go about the process of "True Inner Enlightenment"? Which leads to the question: "How does one express their "Universal Love"? I believe the answer lies within each of us. We begin our journey towards true self–actualization or a higher level of self–consciousness or "Enlightenment" when we begin to discover and learn more about ourselves. This is goal of all rational living beings. We must ultimately find out "who we are". Through that process of self–definition we grow, develop, learn to give, nurture others and are better able to relate to all living beings and ourselves.

Defining Your Purpose

"For whatever things were written before were written for our learning that we through the patience and comfort of the Scriptures might have hope."

Romans 15: 4

Finding out exactly "who" we are can be an exceptionally easy, very difficult, especially challenging, uniquely fluid, or an intensely frustrating process on the road to self–discovery. Personal Growth is the desired outcome that a balanced and healthy person desires. An often–helpful method is to assess the self according to likes, dislikes, gifts, talents, and personality. These tools are methods that guide one to define one's purpose in life.

One may ask, "What is the importance of defining one's purpose?" The answer is quite simple, clarity. Clarity or the gift of "Clear Vision" enables an individual to better see the direction in which they are heading in life. The ability to clearly "see" the path you are walking helps you to avoid obstacles such as stress, anger, frustration, depression, and fear. Clarity also helps you to empower you and aid you in your efforts and endeavors by providing relaxation, comfort, joy, pleasure, powerful self–worth, and a strong sense of responsibility. All of these arenas aid us in determining exactly who we are.

Exactly Who Are You?

"He shall set me up upon a rock."

Psalm 27: 5

We define ourselves by our character traits, our relationship with our environment, and our innate sense of self. Our purpose in life is directly tied to our knowledge of our true self. It is only when our true self manifests itself that we are able to connect with others through love. It is only by getting to know more about one's self that one can take the first steps towards true self–discovery. There are many "self–assessment tools" currently available that one can use to begin the process towards "self learning".

Personality Type Indicators and temperament assessments are measures of common traits that are often displayed and are common to many individuals. It is important to remember that these are just tools. No measure or assessment can truly or comprehensively define the true you. Only you yourself can do this. Only you yourself truly know the true you.

Life as a Path

"I am with thee, and will keep thee in all places whither thou goest."

Genesis 28: 15

If we were to use the metaphor of "Life as a Path" then we openly acknowledge that the events that take place in our lives are meant to be experienced. We acknowledge that we are not here by circumstance but because of a divine purpose. We know that despite the hurt and the pain we are a part of a greater global plan. This is the truth and the basis of "True Enlightenment" and the source of "Universal Love".

Viewing "Life as a Path" aids us in learning to love. It helps us to appreciate one another and the short time that we have here on this planet together. We begin to recognize that sometimes our paths will come together and at other times they will separate and we learn to accept this without envy or regret. We ultimately gain a greater appreciation for all things. It is through this same appreciation that we learn to love each other and the beautiful world that surrounds us.

Everyone Has Skills, Gifts, and Talents

"I will instruct thee and teach thee in the way which thou shalt go."

Psalm 32: 8

It sometimes simply amazes people to know that someone that they know has not one but many varied gifts. It is important to know that everyone has talent in abundance. Everyone has multiple gifts. Often it is an unusual circumstance that leads people to show them. Knowing and utilizing your talents can help one to learn more about the inner–self. Sharing talents with those who appreciate and need them can bring on joy and enhance one's enhance quality of life. I myself learned of a gift that I possess through a most tragic event. It was through such an event that I learned that some gifts despite the circumstances have yet to be uncovered.

Opening Yourself to Learn to Enjoy Life's Ride

"He is able also to save them to the uttermost that come unto God by him."

Hebrews 7: 25

Life is such a multi–changing complex series of events that adapting and surviving can be a challenge in and of itself. However, we as human beings must move beyond the mere mechanisms that are inherent to simple survival. We are here for a purpose. We must recognize this. Identifying our purpose and remaining true to it is the essence of what differentiates us as a life form from the other indigenous beings that inhabit this planet. We must learn to share our love of life by engaging others through respect, caring, and a positive outlook on life referred to as "optimism".

Although it may sound odd to some, optimism and a smile are both healthy and contagious. Having a positive outlook on life can make you an energetic and positive "agent of change". You will begin to witness such a change not only in yourself but also in those around you.

Though few will accept it, attitude can and does make a difference. One must often weigh whether one is taking the "high road" of optimism versus the "low road" of pessimism and negativity. It is not always easy.

Environmental pressures and circumstances often influence and dictate our mood. Becoming optimistic after a tragic event may require a combination of peaceful patience and time to heal. We must remain constantly aware of pessimism. Realizing that pessimism the alternative of optimism can cause painful stress leading to depression, bring about foul moods that can stifle energy, and ultimately put a blanket on innovation, thereby destroying one's ability to create.

It is important to remember that often one's entire outlook can be the deciding factor in determining one's fate. Imagine Captain Ahab of the novel Moby Dick in his relentless and doggedly determined pursuit of the great white whale. It is true that Ahab had awe–inspiring strength, endless drive, and a perseverance that bordered on the superhuman. Yet, despite all of these magnificent attributes Ahab willingly destroyed himself in the end. His pessimistic outlook and passionate pursuit of a fearless animal not only destroyed him but also his ship. Ultimately, Ahab's lack of compassion, understanding, and love led to a negativity that poisoned the fate of his men and ended the lives of all but one of his crew.

Self–Discovery = Walking the Path as Given by Almighty GOD = Enlightenment = Love

"Call unto me, and I will answer thee."

Jeremiah 33: 3

What is love? Almighty GOD is Love. Love is a variety of things that altogether holistically and uniformly manifest themselves as Love. Love is optimism. Love is selflessness. Love is devotion. Love is best defined by action and love is action personified. On "The Road to Self-Discovery" love is the path. Love is the way. Thus we may ask again, "What is love?" Love is in fact, all encompassing. The road to self-discovery is about learning to love oneself. This in turn leads us to learn to appreciate and love others. After all love is... The absolute best that we have to offer one another.

References

Osler, J. E. (2003). The Road to Self–Discovery: Finding One's True Self is the Essence of Enlightenment. The Healing Process: In Need of Counsel. IN: Furstbooks.

CHAPTER: 6

Self-Actualization through Self-Assessment:
Using: *"The Vision Finder © Self-Assessment Tool"*

James E. Osler II, Ed.D.

Conspectus—

The section that follows is a chapter one from the book: **"The Vision Finder the Handheld Edition"**. *"The Vision Finder"* or *"VF"* is a self–assessment tool designed to empower the reader. Chapter One of the book is reprinted here to provide aid the reader in self–assessing themselves to thereby illustrate how important having a written plan of your goals, dreams, skills, gifts, and talents are in the process of self–actualization. The self – actualized scholar is a self–empowered "Entrepreneurial Educator" who follows their written plan to fulfill their divinely given purpose and destiny. Use and enjoy this first chapter of *The Vision Finder:*

CHAPTER

1 THE VISION FINDER
GOALS

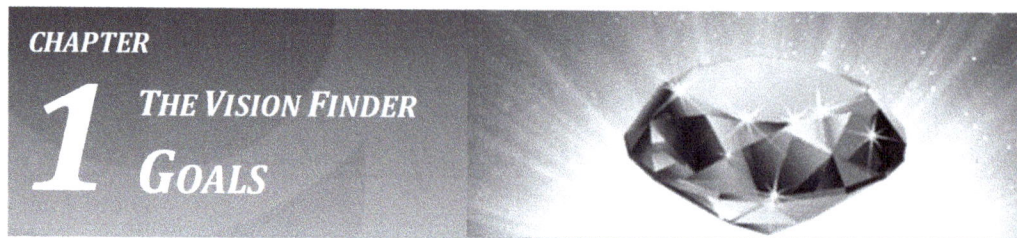

"I will hear what GOD the Lord will speak: for he will speak peace unto his people."

Psalm 85: 8

Hi! I'm Doc Osler better known as "Doc Os" your narrative guide through:

THE **V**ISION **F**INDER™ © Self–Assessment Tool! Let's begin your journey through the Vision Finder by answering a few questions. These questions are designed to get you thinking about your purpose through your present thoughts regarding your career. They will also aid you in creating personal goals and objectives. Complete the following items listed below by filling in the all questions as thoroughly as possible.

Your name:

What do you like about your present profession and/or career?

What do you dislike about your present profession and or career?

Define what you consider to be your talents, gifts, and special abilities?

What are your present (short-term: over the next year) career goals?

What are your (long-term: within the next 5-year) career goals?

What would you describe as your "ideal" or dream career?

If you could do anything of your choosing, what would prefer to be doing at this very moment?

What do you believe is most important in life?

What do you truly care about?

What are you most passionate about?

What is it that you one day Dream of doing (outside of your career)?

How would you go about making your Dream come true?

"Thou shalt call, and I will answer thee."

Job 14: 15

Personal Journal and Chapter Summary

In this section share your thoughts, feelings, and ideas regarding your answers to the Chapter Questions in the space provided.

"I exhort therefore, that, first of all, supplications, prayers, intercessions, and giving of thanks, be made for all men; For kings, and for all that are in authority; that we may lead a quiet and peaceable life in all godliness and honesty. For this is good and acceptable in the sight of God our Saviour; Who will have all men to be saved, and to come unto the knowledge of the truth. For there is one God, and one mediator between God and men, the man Christ Jesus; Who gave himself a ransom for all, to be testified in due time. Whereunto I am ordained a preacher, and an apostle, I speak the truth in Christ, and lie not; a teacher of the Gentiles in faith and verity. I will therefore that men pray everywhere, lifting up holy hands, without wrath and doubting."

1st Timothy 2: 1–8

References

Osler, J. E. (1996). The Effects Of An Ergonomically Designed Computer–Based Tutorial On Elementary Students' Recall. Raleigh, NC: College of Education and Psychology – North Carolina State University.

Osler, J. E. (1996). A Mathematical Equation Expressing the Rectilinear Propulsion of the 100 and 110 Meter Hurdle Races ©. Durham, NC.

Osler, J. E. (2002). University Management Develop Program Comprehensive Report.

Osler, J. E. (2004). Dimensions of Teaching and Behavioral Impediments of Teaching Efficacy. Ideas About Teaching Efficacy: Sharing Perspectives. National Social Sciences Press. Gabe Keri.

Osler, J. E. (2004). The Crisis: Classroom Culture, Identifying and Analyzing Seven Factors That Disable An Effective Collegiate Teaching Methodology. A Long Way to Go: Conversations About Race By African American Faculty And Students. Peter Lang.

Osler, J. E. (2005) Technology Engineering: A Paradigm Shift In The Dynamics of Instruction; A New Philosophy of Education For Teaching In The Information Age. 2005 The South Atlantic Philosophy of Education Society Refereed 50th Conference.

Osler, J. E. (2005). Creating An Interactive Cognitive Economy: The Use of an Asynchronous Learning Network Course Management System to Develop an Interactive Community of Learners. Research Paper for 2005 The South Atlantic Philosophy of Education Society Refereed 50th Conference.

Osler, J. E. (2005). Technology Engineering: Developing, Implementing, and Infusing Interactive Metametric Learning Modules into an Asynchronous Learning Network to Develop an Interactive Community of Learners. Research Paper for The 2005 South Atlantic Philosophy of Education Society Refereed 50th Conference.

Osler, J. E. (2010). THE VISION FINDER ©. The Handheld Edition. Durham, NC: Publishing Division, Osler Studios Incorporated[™]©.

Osler, J. E. (2010). VISUALUS [™] © Visioneering Volumetrically: The Mathematics of the Innovative Problem–Solving Model of Inventive Instructional Design. Durham, NC: Publishing Division, Osler Studios Incorporated[™]©.

Osler, J. E. (2010). PERCEPTOLOGY [™] © The Science of Comprehension that is Universal Instructional Design through Visualus, Metacognetic Mechanics, Technology Engineering, and Optimal Instruction. Durham, NC: Publishing Division, Osler Studios Incorporated [™] ©.

Osler, J. E. (2012). The Vision Finder™ © E–Book: An Assessment Designed to Determine Purpose and Fulfill Destiny by Unlocking Unlimited Potential (1st ed.). OSI © in partnership with Apple iBooks, Silicon Valley, CA.

Osler, J. E. (2018). The Vision Finder™ © E–Book: The New Handheld Edition (New ed.). OSI © in partnership with Morrisville, NC: Lulu Publications.

Osler, J. E. (2018). The Vision Finder™ ©: The New Handheld Edition (New ed.). OSI © in partnership with Morrisville, NC: Lulu Publications.

CHAPTER: 7 *Exploding HBCU Culture Pathology Part Six: Changing the Culture and Environment Through Research*

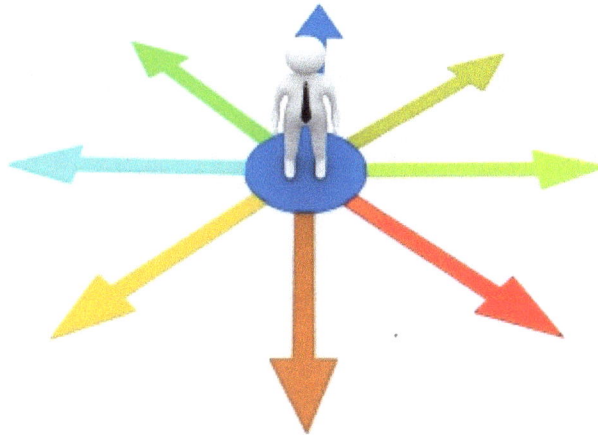

An Assessment Designed to Assess Faculty Involvement: Determining Faculty Shared Governance in Institutions of Higher Learning

The following questionnaire/survey instrument was designed to assess and determine the level of faculty attitudes and perceptions related to shared governance and leadership in higher institutions. The results are designed to be used to develop means of improving institutional and Faculty Professional Development. Faculty participation was voluntary and all answers were anonymous. If Faculty chose to participate in the survey, they had the opportunity to withdraw their consent at any time. Faculty addressed the items in the questionnaire by placing an (×) in the box or space that was provided that best represented their response to the stated question (according to the item that corresponded with an opportunity to mark off an answer). If Faculty had any questions about the survey or any specific questions, they were instructed to contact: Dr. Masila Mutisya or Dr. M. Michaux Parker.

This section of the survey is designed to assess the current level of collegially at your institution. Please place and (X) in the box that best represents your response to the statement.

No.	Item:	Strongly Disagree	Disagree	Agree	Strongly Agree
1.	The relationship between the administration and faculty senate/council is collegial.	O	O	O	O
2.	The relationship between non-senate faculty and faculty senators/council representative is collegial.	O	O	O	O
3.	The relationship between the administration and staff senate is collegial.	O	O	O	O
4.	The relationship between the administration and non-senate staff is collegial.	O	O	O	O
5.	The relationship between the administration and undergraduate students is collegial.	O	O	O	O
6	The relationship between the administration and graduate students is collegial.	O	O	O	O
7.	The relationship between the faculty and undergraduate students.	O	O	O	O
8.	The relationship between the faculty and graduate students.	O	O	O	O

No.	Item:	Strongly Disagree	Disagree	Agree	Strongly Agree
9.	Faculty senate has a powerful position in influencing the university's agenda.	O	O	O	O
10.	Faculty senate has a powerful position in influencing educational policy.	O	O	O	O
11.	Faculty senate has a powerful position in enforcing administrative accountability.	O	O	O	O
12.	Faculty senate has a powerful position in creating university mandates.	O	O	O	O

13.	What are the three (3) most common issues that face your institution regarding shared governance?

_____

_____

_____

14.	What changes should be made in order to promote increased shared governance at your institution? Please write comments below:

_____

_____

_____

This section of the survey is designed to assess the current perceptions of administrative officers at your institution. Please place and (X) in the box or space that best represents your response to the stated question.

No.	Item:	Strongly Disagree	Disagree	Agree	Strongly Agree
15.	The administration is in-touch with university problems.	O	O	O	O
16.	The administration consults faculty senate, faculty on university matters prior to making decisions.	O	O	O	O
17.	The administration takes faculty senate/faculty concerns seriously.	O	O	O	O
18.	The administration has a genuine interest in shared governance.	O	O	O	O
19.	The administration has a genuine respect for the faculty.	O	O	O	O
20.	The university administrators are open to change.	O	O	O	O
21.	Faculty senate and the administration have mutual respect for one another.	O	O	O	O
22.	Faculty senate and the administration have mutual trust.	O	O	O	O
23.	Faculty senate and the administration have mutual openness with each other (Transparency).	O	O	O	O
24.	Faculty senate and the administration have an equal partnership in governance in protecting Academic Freedom.	O	O	O	O
25.	As a faculty member, I am a leader within my department/ academic unit.	O	O	O	O

26.	As a faculty member, I am a leader within the university at large.	O	O	O	O
27.	As a faculty member, I am a leader within my academic discipline/ field.	O	O	O	O

Demographics:

28.	Ethnicity	O African-American	O White
		O Asian	O Other
		O Hispanic	
29.	Gender	O Female	O Male
30.	Years in Academia	____	____
31.	Years at your institution	____	
32.	Academic Position	O Faculty- Tenured	O Faculty- Tenure Track
		O Faculty- Adjunct	O Administrator and Faculty
		O Administrator	O Other_____
33.	Faculty Senator	O Yes	O No

34.	Governance	O Governed by Faculty Senate
		O Governed by Faculty Council
		O Governed by other. (Specify)
		_____
35.	Institution	O Public O Private
36.	Years in existence	_____
37.	Has Tenure and Promotion processes	O Yes O No

Your participation is helping to improve shared governance for your institution.

THANK YOU

References

Mutisya P. M. & Parker M. M. (2012). A Survey to Determine Faculty Attitudes and Perceptions Related to Shared Governance and Leadership in Higher Education Institutions.

CHAPTER: 8	Exploding HBCU Culture Pathology Part Seven: Creating Gender Equity in the Professorate and In the Community Using Paulo Freire's Conscientização Model

Marginalization of Women from the Professorate to the Community; How Do We Begin to Address the Problem—The Answer: A Philosophical Approach to Understanding Women and Global Empowerment Using Paulo Freire's Model

Philliph M. Mutisya and James E. Osler II

Conspectus—

Most discussions on understanding global world view that impacts social dynamics in most societies and identity issues pertaining to societal development and socialization of women and men usually are devoid of the woman voice although men use the women passive voice that tent to make the woman role in sharing power, raising children, and leadership role, is usually perceived as a sub-set of the man and on either or dichotomy in thinking. This chapter attempts to frame a discussion on how we are socialized as women and men from a global worldview and how the world has continued to become a Global Village but the women voce still remains marginal to the center of intellectuals and power sharing. In this chapter we propose a methodological approach based on critical dialogue approach that apply Critical Theories in terms of Philosophical Approach to Understanding Women role in socialization women and men from a global view. The world and global view in any society shapes how women view and are viewed and their impact on the social, political, economic, and identity. How we understand the woman role in our societies that are not only diverse but multicultural, impact the culture and empowerment and how we value women in general. In this chapter we explore theoretical and conceptual aspects that may be useful in empowering women from a Global Empowerment perspective applying Paulo Freire Model on Critical Conscious Approach to dialogue (Conscientização). The rationale of framing the discussion on Women Empowerment from a global perspective is to raise awareness on the critical role of a woman in conceptualizing a critical dialogue that includes women voice in decision-making differently from most traditional ways that have silenced and suppressed women role in socialization leading to global and world conflicts in identity and socialization.

Key Words: *Global Worldview, Internalized Oppression, Conscientização, Praxis, Philosophical Analysis, Philosophical Cultural Differences, Empowerment.*

Introduction

Understanding philosophical approach in the way women are viewed from global world view is an undertaking that not only is challenging but is also very systemic and rather complex. This is because of the long history and diversity and complexity of world experiences. However, in order to frame an in-depth and coherent epistemological approach requires a reflective analysis that informs and formulates a conceptual experience that shapes our consciousness. Thus, the framing and reframing of the issues that emerge to form conclusions and actions that are the means to develop the foundation of understanding of women in terms of "Global Empowerment". We first have to define the process and in doing so thereby identify conceptual models that shape our understanding of how any society shapes the psyche of people in a coexisting space.

According Dr. Nayef R.F. Al-Rodhan & Ambassador Gerard Stoudmann, in the Geneva Centre for Security Policy (2006), they define "Globalization as a process that encompasses the cause, course, and consequences of transnational and transcultural integration of human and non-human activities" (Al-Rodhan & Stoudmann, 2006). Thus, when addressing the philosophical and psychological aspects that shape our global view, it is imperative to set the foundation of the theoretical approach and the conceptualization of the main issues that shape our understanding. However, the understanding of how we view the world has to be derived from the perspective of social and behavioral science. This view is shared by the field of "Community Psychology" as a linking science. Al-Rodhan & Stoudmann (2006) asserts that, "it is not the relation between the individual and society, but the relation between the individual, community, and society". Therefore, recognizing the diversity of its local or regional agendas, can help in studying and understanding social problems from their subsumed human relational realities. It can contribute also to the knowledge and comprehension of individual subjective and objective situations related to healthy and unhealthy behaviors and mental conditions. Thus, the "Global World View" is not about just understanding international experience but how international aspects shape one's local and national view (thus this leads to a rational understanding of how local becomes international in the following manner from: local to→regional to→national to→international).

This is to say that the concept and reality of community imply not only a mediating role in the exchanges between the individual and society, but that it becomes, in some sense, a third important element in order to explain and understand the status and dynamics of the human condition: relationality, communication, conversation (that are altogether "trichotomous" see Osler, 2017 for an in-depth definition of trichotomy from a scientific framework). In framing the dialogue on understanding "Philosophical Approach to Understanding Women and Global Empowerment" the analysis has to be framed from a critical point of view. According to Stevens, P. L., and Bean. T.W. (2007), states that "Critical literacy is concerned with critiquing relationship among language use, social practice, and power (sharing). It is an analytic process that is mediated by one's worldview or theory and that closely examines the way in which language practices carve up the world according to certain socially valued criteria (and not other sets of criteria)". Thus, critical literacy theory is concerned with inequities and advocates for rethinking of the ideas and social assumptions that are viewed as natural or unassailable. According to Stevens & Bean (2007) critical literacy theory is rooted in philosophy, linguistics and discourse studies (trichotomous [philosophy; linguistics; discourse] as opposed to dichotomous which shapes the identity of a people or a person or a cultural identity (also trichotomous—people; person; and culture). The formulation of the discourse about the aforementioned can be found in the work of Paulo Freire. However, Paulo Freire's work as translated by Donald Macedo (2005) and Ira Shor (1987) (both identified in Stygall's 1989, "Teaching Freire in North America: A Review Essay of Ira Shor's Freire for the Classroom: A Sourcebook for Liberatory Teaching") makes the foundation of the critical literacy theory as a distinct theoretical and pedagogical field.

Stevens & Bean (2007) provides a rationale for critical literacy by asserting that "in this era of increased globalization demands an informed decision making in order to navigate through the world landscape that has become more interconnected in communication through the use of technology and as such the world is more flat than it is perceived a round as indicated by Thomas Friedman in 2005 in the Pulitzer Prize winning book "The World is Flat: A Brief History of the Twenty-First Century". Stevens & Bean (2007) also points out that, "the era of technological and Information Age creates unavoidable realities that mandate education process to change into transformative and transformational approach that leverages the resources available or at our disposal and use the tools that allow us as citizens to survive the rapid speed and growth in which the tools and the language are changing". They further state that, "We are entering a phase where we are going to see the digitization, virtualization, and automation of everything". Stevens & Bean gives an example of such rapid changes by citing how the electronic version of the Wikipedia encyclopedia has outpaced the printed versions (p. xiii), which requires citizenry to acquire well-rounded education and well equipped with critical literacy to be able offer insightful and accurate critique of information and communication (Stevens & Bean, 2007).

To understand philosophical and psychological aspects that shapes cultural identity and how women are shaped by the way the society views them it is imperatives to analyze the historical and sociological phenomenon that make the basis of the foundation of philosophical and psychological world view and identity as a functional aspect in existing in a society. In such examination and applying critical theory, the analysis has to be informed in examining philosophical analysis by looking at Philosophical Cultural Differences. Philosophical Analysis is an emerging approach to understanding cultural identity and world view that leads to global awareness.

The Conscientização Process – Paulo Freire (1994, 1996 & 2014)

Paulo Freire, through his work in the slums of Brazil, began to conceptualize a process of conscious-raising leading toward a dynamic concept of liberation and towards what he refers to as a more complete humanness. The product of this process he called: **"Conscientização"** (Freire, 1996 & 2014). Conscientização ("Critical Conscious Approach to Dialogue"), is an approach designed to engage participants to develop a level of consciousness that enables them to see social systems critically. Participants are able to perceive and understand the contradictions that affect their lives arising from educational, economic, social, and political forces, and to generalize those contradictions to others around them (Freire, 1994, and Smith, 1975). The outcome of the process is a heightened awareness that leads to self-awareness as empowerment process, and developing competencies on Knowledge, Skills and dispositions for effective culturally responsive facilitation in diverse cultural contexts. In essence, the participants learn to know themselves before engaging and making judgments about others from ethnic, racial, genders, and cultures, or economic backgrounds. Additionally, the following is true of the "Conscientização Process":

- A degree of consciousness in which individuals are able to see the social system critically. They are able to understand the resultant contradictions in their own lives, to generalize those contradictions to others around them and transform society creatively with others. The process is coded into three levels: Magical, Naïve and Critical.

- *Naming:*
  What are the most pressing problems in your life or in your teaching profession right now? Should things be as they are? How should they be? (relate these questions to the problems you find in your profession that are dehumanizing or impact your work negatively.

- *Reflecting:*
  Why are things this way?
  Who is to blame?
  What is your role in the situation?

- *Acting:*
  What can be done?
  What should be done?
  What have you done or will you do?

The process involves reflecting on one's thinking and taking appropriate action that all humans need to use to change the internalized mindset and world view. This exercise is effective when addressed at individual level and then generalize to group or society level. The significance of the model is that, it prepares you to take appropriate action without blaming self or others and taking responsibility of your own mindset and the change you want to see.

Other Models Designed for Change of Internalized Oppression: The Jackson and Hardiman Model of Social Identity Development, 1997

The generic social identity development theory is an adaptation of black identity development theory (Jackson, 1976) and white identity development theory (Hardiman, 1982).2 Social identity development theory has also been influenced by other theorists and applications to other social groups (Cross, 1971, 1978, 1991; Helms, 1990; Kim, 1981; Schapiro, 1985). Social identity development theory describes attributes that are common to the identity development process for members of all target and agent groups. We present the stages, for purposes of conceptual clarity, as if a person were to move neatly from one stage to the next. In reality most people experience several stages simultaneously, holding complex perspectives on a range of issues and living a mixture of social identities. This developmental model can be helpful in understanding student perspectives and selecting instructional strategies, but we caution against using it simplistically to label people.

Includes responding to triggers that shape the oppressive mindset. A trigger is something that an individual says or does or an organizational policy or practice that makes us, as members of social groups, feel diminished, offended, threatened, stereotyped, discounted or attacked. Triggers do not necessarily threaten our physical safety. We often feel psychologically threatened. We can also be triggered on behalf of another social group. Though we do not feel personally threatened, our sense of social justice is violated. Triggers cause an emotional response. These emotions range from hurt, confusion, anger, fear, surprise or embarrassment. We respond to triggers in a variety of ways, some helpful and others not. Our guide in developing a full repertoire of responses to triggers is to take care of ourselves and then decide how to most effectively respond. Some of the responses listed here are effective and some are not. What responses we choose depends on our own inner resources and the dynamics of the situation. This list is not intended to be all-inclusive and is in no order of preference. The list of responses are as follows: Leave; Avoidance; Silence; Release; Attack; Internalization; Rationalization; Confusion; Shock; Name/Naming; Confront; Surprise; Strategize; Misinterpretation; and Discretion. Read the list of responses in the section that follows and think about the discussion questions at the end of the list.

The List of Trigger Responses from the Jackson and Hardiman Model (1997)

LEAVE: We physically remove ourselves from the triggering situation.

AVOIDANCE: We avoid future encounters with and withdraw emotionally from people or situations that trigger us.

SILENCE: We do not respond to the triggering situation though we feel upset by it. We endure the situation without saying or doing anything.

RELEASE: We notice the trigger, but do not take it in. We choose to let it go. We do not feel the need to respond.

ATTACK: We respond with an intention to hurt or offend whoever has triggered us.

INTERNALIZATION: We internalize the trigger. We believe it to be true.

RATIONALIZATION: We convince ourselves that we misinterpreted the trigger, that the intention was not to hurt us, or that we tell ourselves we are overreacting so that we can avoid saying anything about the trigger.

CONFUSION: We feel upset but are not clear about why we feel that way. We know we feel angry, hurt or offended. We just don't know what to say or do about it.

SHOCK: We are caught off guard, unprepared to be triggered by this person or situation and have a difficult time responding. (Teaching for Diversity and Social Justice ©, Second Edition, Routledge, 2007)

NAME: We identify what is upsetting us to the triggering person or organization. We name the trigger and invite discussion about it with the triggering person or organization.

CONFRONT: We name the trigger and demand that the offending behavior or policy be changed.

SURPRISE: We respond to the trigger in an unexpected way. For example, we react with constructive humor that names the trigger, but makes people laugh.

STRATEGIZE: We work with others to develop a programmatic or political intervention to address the trigger in a larger context.

MISINTERPRETATION: We are feeling on guard and expect to be triggered so that we misinterpret something someone says and are triggered by our misinterpretation rather than by what they actually said.

DISCRETION: Because of dynamics in the situation (power differences, risk of physical violence or retribution, for example), we decide that it is not in our best interests to respond to the trigger at that time, but choose to address the trigger in some other way at another time.

Jackson and Hardiman Model (1997) Discussion Questions

Which responses are most typical for you when you are triggered?

As a targeted group member?

As an advantaged group member?

Are there differences in how you respond to triggers depending on the "ism"?

Which responses would you like to add to your repertoire?

Which responses do you use now and would like to stop using or use more selectively?

What blocks you from responding to triggers in ways that feel more effective?

What can you do to expand your response repertoire?

Another model that involves metacognition and self-reflective analysis is Philosophical Cultural Differences – Edwin J. Nichols (1981 & 1990). This model engages individuals to explore the sources of bias and oppressive conditioning in socialization. The reflection on one's beliefs and how they see and interact with the world in generalization and responding to others. Philosophical cultural differences help individuals to analyze their experience in the world and to understand who they are and how to interpret the world and how the world interacts with them. The model helps individuals to examine their beliefs and how they have been influenced by other beliefs either from Eurocentric world view which is based on dichotomous things or Either/Or logic in thinking and how this world views and beliefs shapes one's identity and copying. Afrocentric worldview is shaped by "Triple Heritage" (Ala Amin Mazrui, 1986 and 2007) which is shaped by Either/Or and Other (Either/Or + Other) which holistic and inclusive of all heritages, Africa-South East and North.

When we speak of community in this narrative, we refer to a form of group relationship based on a dynamic interaction relatively stable that includes strategies of conflict management and diverse levels of shared utopias. In other words, we have in mind a collective process of an evolving system of stabilized relationships, of a dynamic network of communication, of a web of ongoing conversations among individuals in which they can find mutuality, affection and identity. Community as relationality adopts different community structures according to historical and cultural circumstances and places. The Third International Conference on Community Psychology (1998) was designed to build knowledge on the way diverse community structures and experiences approach and confront the four main concerns of our times (Marsella, 1998).

A proposal to enlarge the field is offered by Wolfgang Stark (2012) in "Community Psychology as a Linking Science: Potentials and Challenges for Transdisciplinary Competencies". Community Psychology must go beyond its traditional concerns and its focus on local communities. The idea includes collaborating more with other disciplines, societal institutions, business companies; learning from different cultural values approaches; focusing on macro and micro issues of community analysis and community building; developing its identity as a linking science (Stark, 2012). In "The War Without Bullets: Socio-structural Violence from a Critical Standpoint" David Frye (2012), a community psychologist, and Cathy McCormack (2012), a community activist, have worked in mutually supportive and stimulating ways to collaboratively understand and contest socio-structural violence (Fryer & McCormack, 2012). They focused critically on interconnections between poverty, inequality, unemployment and psycho-social destruction. The community activist characterized these interconnections as manifestations of "War Without Bullets" waged against oppressed people. She has promoted awareness. The community psychologist has tried to develop the notion of a "War Without Bullets" to give it theoretical discursive legitimacy (Fryer & McCormack, 2012 & 2013).

In the "Principles of African Environmental Ethics" author Ibanga (2018) identifies five principles of African environmental ethics drawn from the wide corpus of African environmental ethics. These are precepts or injunctions designed to guide the behaviour of people in the environment. Ibanga (2018) states that "the principles call for restraint and circumspection in decision-making and action-taking such that one's lifestyle, behaviour and dealings can lead to avoidance of wastage of resources and minimize injuries caused other beings (humans and nonhumans) and their communities (culture, ecosystem, etc.)." In other words, the principles serve as a context to anticipate before acting. In addition, they serve as a guide to researchers when they analyze and interpret data collected in African environmental ethics research. They provide the following:

- Principle of Accommodation: Act in such a way that nonhuman existents and future people are considered and accommodated in your daily decisions and   dealings.
- Principle of Gratitude: Act in such a way that reflects your gratitude towards other existents, humans and nonhumans, for contributing to support your "beingness" or existence.
- Principle of Restoration: Always act to restore to Nature the loss you have caused it. For example, re-planting a tree after felling one.
- Principle of Control: Act in such a way that you control your action from producing too much negative externalities.
- Principle of Necessity: Act only on decisions and actions that are absolutely necessary.

References

Al-Rodhan, N. R., & Stoudmann, G. (2006). Definitions of globalization: A comprehensive overview and a proposed definition. *Program on the Geopolitical Implications of Globalization and Transnational Security*, 6(1-21).

Freire, P. (1994). Pedagogy of hope: Reliving pedagogy of the oppressed, trans. *Robert R. Baar, notes Ana Maria Araújo Freire (New York: Continuum, 2004), 77.*

Freire, P. (1996). Pedagogy of the oppressed (revised). *New York: Continuum.*

Freire, P., & Macedo, D. (2005). *Literacy: Reading the word and the world.* Routledge.

Freire, P. (2014). Education and Conscientização. *Education for Adults, 1,* 279-92.

Friedman, Thomas L. *The World is Flat: A brief history of the twenty-first century.* New York: Farrar, Straus and Giroux, 2005.

Fryer, D., & McCormack, C. (2012). The war without bullets: Socio-structural violence from a critical standpoint. *Global Journal of Community Psychology Practice, 3*(1), 87-92.

Fryer, D., & McCormack, C. (2013). Special section editorial: Psychology and poverty reduction. *The Australian Community Psychologist, 25*(1), 7-12.

Griffin, P., & Harro, B. (2002). Teaching for diversity and social justice: A source book.

Hardiman, R. (1997). Jackson and Hardiman model of social identity development. *Teaching for diversity and social justice: A sourcebook,* 22-39.

Hardiman R. & B. W. Jackson (1997), Conceptual foundations for social justice courses, in M. Adams, L. A. Bell, P. Griffin (Eds.), Teaching for diversity and social justice: A sourcebook (New York: Routledge), pp. 23-29. Citations refer to the 1997 edition.

Ibanga, D. A. (2018). Concept, Principles and Research Methods of African Environmental Ethics.

Marsella, A. J. (1998). Toward a "global-community psychology": Meeting the needs of a changing world. *American psychologist, 53*(12), 1282.

Mazrui, A. A. (1986). *The Africans: A Triple Heritage – A Companion Volume to the 9-Part Documentary Series.* A book that was published as a part of the documentary series jointly produced by the BBC and the Public Broadcasting Service (WETA, Washington) in association with the Nigerian Television Authority.

Mazrui, A. A. (2007). Between Secular Activism and Religious Observance: Abu Mayanja and Africa's Triple Heritage. *Abu Mayanja Memorial Lecture, Kampala, Uganda, July, 30.*

Mutisya, P. M. (2020). Trialogue. Discussions about psychological mindset. School of Education, North Carolina Central University.

Mutisya, P. M. & Osler, J. E. (2020). Trialogue: "The Diaspora of Philosophical Cultural Differences Model". School of Education, North Carolina Central University.

Nichols, E. J. (1981). *Philosophical aspects of cultural differences.* Western Psychiatric Institute and Clinic.

Nichols, E. J. (1990). Presentation: *Philosophical aspects of cultural differences.* From Western Psychiatric Institute and Clinic presented at North Carolina State University in the College of Education and Psychology.

Parkay, F. W., Stanford, B. H., & Gougeon, T. D. (2010). *Becoming a teacher* (pp. 432-462). Pearson/Merrill.

Osler, J. E. (2018). Trioengineering Interapplication and Comprehensive Cohesive Cogitation: The Use of Systemic Neuromathematical Trioinformatics to Create, Define, and Express Trichotomous Research Instrumentation and Tri–Squared Analytics. *July–September i-manager's Journal on Mathematics, 7* (3), pp. 10–29.

Osler, J. E. (2017). Triology: A Novel, Innovative, and In–Depth Science Concerned with the Mathematical Triadic, Tripartite, and Triplex Components, Content, and Cycles of Life, Learning, Logic, and the Universal Aspects of Nature. *i-manager's January–March Journal on Mathematics, 6* (1), pp. 1–17.

Osler, J. E. (2015). Neuroengineering Neuromathematics Notation: The Novel Trioinformatics System that Defines, Explains, and Expresses the Research Application of the Law of Trichotomy for Digital Instrumentation and Circuit Design. *i-manager's June–August Journal on Circuits and Systems, 3* (3), pp. 1–16.

Shor, I. (1987). *Freire for the classroom: A sourcebook for liberatory teaching.* Heinemann Educational Books, Inc., 70 Court St., Portsmouth, NH 03801.

Smith, W. A. (1975). Conscientização: an operational definition. Dissertation University of Massachusetts at Amherst.

Stark, W. (2012). Community Psychology as a Linking Science Potentials and Challenges for Transdisciplinary Competences. *Global Journal of Community Psychology Practice, 3*(1).

Stevens, L. P., & Bean, T. W. (2007). *Critical literacy: Context, research, and practice in the K-12 classroom.* Sage Publications.

Stygall, G. (1989). Teaching Freire in North America: A Review Essay of Ira Shor's Freire for the Classroom: A Sourcebook for Liberatory Teaching. *Journal of Teaching Writing, 8*(1), 113-126.

Wijeyesinghe, C. L., & Jackson III, B. W. (2001). *New Perspectives on Racial Identity Development: A Theoretical and Practical Anthology.* New York University Press, Orders and Customer Service, 838 Broadway, 3rd Floor, New York, NY 10003-4812 (paperback: ISBN-0-8147-9343-6; hardback: ISBN-0-8147-9342-8).

		Exploding HBCU Culture Pathology Part Eight: Metacognetic Mechanics to Deconstruct and Define All Manifested Forms of Oppression
CHAPTER:	9	

—Holistically Using Metacognetic Mechanics to Impactfully and Effectively Deconstruct and Define Any and All Manifested Forms of Oppression—

By

James Edward Osler II

Conspectus—

The HBCU had its origins and indeed its inception in the Black Church which was the center of the Black community. As HBCUs at present by and large are disappearing it is time that they *"return to their first love"*. That is to say, Jesus Christ and His Church in particular. This particular Chapter as a monograph provides an active discourse on the identification, functions, interrelationships, manifestations, and solution to negative human behaviors that are often seen as a result of oppression. This treatise quantifies human behavioral patterns through the use of parsimonious abbreviations to create novel mathematical formulae which are the logic statements new notations, innovative models, and idealistic operations that explain (in detail) and ultimately resolve the human interaction differences via definable rational arithmetic methodologies. It also extends the research that initially appeared in the author's book entitled "Visualus™ ©" written in 2010. The neuroscientific terminology for the manifested negative human behavioral patterns was provided via discussions with a prominent educational researcher and noted athletic coach whom through their own varied life-long experiences provided the author with a wealth of detailed information that was clearly defined and is now contextually resubmitted to now appear in this particular text. It is the author's hope that by shedding light on the negative manifested behaviors and providing an active positive solution that in the future healing can occur and delivery from all of the ramifications of the negative aspects of any form of manifested oppression.

Keywords: Crabs in the Bucket Syndrome, Internalized Oppression, Interposition Nullification, Manifested Human Behavior, Metacognetic Mechanics, Neuropsychosocial, Philopsychosocial, Physiosocial, Psychophysiosocial, Oppression, and Trichotomy.

Introduction

This narrative provides an epistemological rationale for the identification, functions, interrelationships, and ultimately provides a solution to the negative aspects of human behavior that so often plague relationships (whether they are interpersonal, professional, or indirect). The human behaviors outlined in this narrative that are often manifested as the direct result of oppression. Oppression in this sense can be traumatic as the result of an experience or most likely ongoing experiences that deliver regular continual pressure on the individual (or individuals) that can be: mental, physical, social, emotional, and/or spiritual or a combination of any of the aforementioned. This paper in the sections that follow will actively define and by doing so accurately quantifies human behavioral patterns through the use of parsimonious abbreviations to create novel mathematical formulae. These formulae will serve as the substantive logic statements that will provide a series of new notations for innovative models as idealistic operations that explain and detail the outcome of negative human behavior openly manifested due to ongoing oppression. The end of the paper ultimately resolves the human interaction difficulties due to oppression by providing the solution to the aforesaid defined arithmetic methodologies. In due course, the research and outcomes presented here greatly extends the initial research by the author first completed presented in 2010.

Broadening the Initial Definition of "Metacognetic Mechanics"

The term "Metacognetic Mechanics" was first introduced in the authors 2010 book entitled "Visualus™ © Visioneering Volumetrically: The Mathematics of The Innovative Problem-Solving Model of Inventive Instructional Design" (Osler, 2010). In the book Visualus, the term "Metacognetic" was initially defined in the following manner: *"By collaboratively combining the terms "Meta"* (meaning "beyond", "after" or "higher level") *and "Cognetic"* (meaning "thoughts that pertain to a particular action") *the new term "Metacognetic" is created. Metacognetic is defined as "forward–thinking beneficial thoughts that create purposeful meaningful solutions in the learning environment"* (using the Innovative Problem–Solving Model of Inventive Instructional Design). When the term becomes plural (as "Metacognetics") it now becomes a discipline. "Metacognetics" is defined as "The discipline of creating instructional delivery methods that go beyond traditional instructional techniques by employing innovative instructional strategies" (Osler, 2010). Similarly, the term "Mechanics" was defined in Visualus in this manner: "Mechanics" is the branch of physics concerned with the behavior of physical bodies. The discipline of Physics originated with Mechanics. Physics is grounded in Mechanics which provides an extensive body of knowledge about the natural world. The study of Mechanics is also a central part of Technology which is defined in Metacognetic Mechanics as the capability of human beings to practically apply knowledge to produce crafts, systems, and tools that allow society to better interact with the environment. In Metacognetic Mechanics, the term "Mechanics" applies to "Engineering" or "Applied Mechanics" and directly refers to the Technology Engineering methodology" (Osler, 2010).

Metacognetic Mechanics was initially defined in Visualus as follows: "The terminology "Metacognetic Mechanics" literally represents the bridging of the two distinct terms "Metacognetic" and "Mechanics" into a new collaborative whole. Metacognetic Mechanics © broadens the scope of the term "Metacognetics" by placing emphasis on how to produce solutions in the learning environment. These solutions are produced through the use of interactive instructional tools collaboratively combined with optimally effective instruction" (Osler, 2010). In expanding "Metacognetic Mechanics" from its initial more technical definition to a more global definition that more accurately describes human patterns of behavior, it can now be more broadly defined as follows:

"Metacognetic Mechanics is defined as forward-thinking beneficial thoughts that create purposeful meaningful tangible solutions manifested through positive outcomes as a result of positive intentional physical behavior".

In terms of this paper, Metacognetic Mechanics under the new definition is used to create forward-thinking solutions as definitions, terminologies, and mathematical models designed to deconstruct and define all manifested forms of oppression and its outcomes exemplified as negative human patterns of behavior. Thus, Metacognetic Mechanics (in terms of human behavior) is the "Tripositive" (or "Trichotomously Triple Positive" = "$+_{[1]}{}^{[+]} +_{[2]}{}^{[+]} +_{[3]}$"; "Triple +" = $[+3]+ = "Tri\Sigma"$) solution. This solution occurs through a cognitive dissonance in which the focus of the oppressed transitions from him or herself to a metaphysical reality beyond the scope of their personal suffering from manifested oppression. In this manner, they are healed and become whole because their entire focus is now on something and someone greater whose entire purpose is to relieve them of their oppression.

Definitions of Manifested Human Behavior: Defining Trichotomous and Dichotomous Dynamic Behavioral Patterns in Terms of Human Interaction

The following terminology is designed to provide accurate descriptions of the outcomes that are manifested as "negative human behavior". In addition, there are new definitions of the interplay and interaction of known human behavioral sciences that can best describe the relationships between the mind, the body, the emotions and the interactions that occur between terminologies that exist as outcomes due to ongoing oppression. These novel terms are defined and described in deference to the primary aim of this paper which is to deconstruct and define the outcomes of manifested oppression that directly damage human interactions due to negative behavioral patterns.

The terms that are associated with detrimental negative human behavioral patterns are identified as follows:

(a.) "Neuropsychosocial" this term is a trichotomous portmanteau from the three terms "Neurological"; "Physiological"; and "Social". Together these three combined terms were created by the author to define "biological human brain functions" + "mentality" + "person-to-person interaction" that are functioning framework for a particular learned behavior. It this narrative it is used to describe the overall learned behavioral outcome as a result of the trichotomous summation that is the direct combination of: negative "Philopsychosocial" behavior + negative "Physiosocial" behavior + negative "Psychophysiosocial" behavior. "Neuropsychosocial" in this discourse actively describes the negative "mind-self-thought" process that is encumbered by self-marginalization brought about by a trifold of negative behavioral factors as a result of perpetual external oppression. Thus, negative "Neuropsychosocial" behavior in this narrative is described and defined to be "Negative Justification".

(b.) "Psychophysiosocial" this term is also a portmanteau from the three terms "Psychological"; "Physiological"; and "Social". This new term was created by the author into an innovative trichotomous whole to explain the combination of human: "Mentality" + "internal body physical reaction" + "person-to-person interaction"

(c.) "Philopsychosocial" the last three term portmanteau in this narrative is a combination of "Philosophical"; "Psychological"; and "Social". This terminology was created by noted educational and social science researcher, Dr. Philliph Masila Mutisya to illustrate the theoretical framework that describes in detail the "conceptualization" + "mental gymnastics" + "person-to-person interaction" that formulates the particulars of internally centralized human behavior. An ideal example of this is Dr. Mutisya's notion of **"Internalized Oppression"** which describes the idea, mentality, and social dynamics of negative human behavior as a result of internally adopting the external oppressive pressures inflicted on an individual.

(d.) "Physiosocial" the only double termed portmanteau in this treatise on human behavior. It is combined from the dual terms: "Physiological" and "Social" into a novel whole. This new term was created by the author similar to the others to describe the ideal negative behavior so well defined by the late well-renowned athletic coach Wilbur Ross in conversations during the late 20th Century with the author. "Physiosocial" is described here as the overall descriptor for one of three negative human behaviors that concerns a level of physical "negation with no relation to the present situation". This is best described as physical "oppositional" human behavior or "oppression operationalized through external antisocial competition". An example is accurately definitive derogatory term for "proactively getting in the way of another as they attempt to establish interpersonal relationship with another

person" more commonly referred to as *"cock-blocking"*, idealistically defined here by the terms **"Interposition Nullification"**.

(e.) "Negative Justification" which are two distinct terms that combined by the author describe the negative human behavioral need to seek self-justification through negative validation by an oppressor. Negative Justification is simply operationalized Triological Science—"Trinegation" which is the negative joint summation of three negative behavioral factors or behavioral patterns that are "internal" (created from outside oppression that becomes detrimentally individually internalized) + "oppositional" (oppression operationalized through external antisocial competition) + external (outside oppression that manifests as external mutually destructive behavior) they are: . "Negative Justification" is a form of manifested negative "Neuropsychosocial" behavior that is extremely detrimental to individual development as it is steeped in the dual negative effects of "low self-esteem" and "low self-worth".

(f.) "Internalized Oppression" a notion espoused by Dr. Philliph Mutisya that describes the idea, mentality, and social dynamics of negative human behavior as a result of internally adopting the external oppressive pressures inflicted on an individual. "Internalized Oppression" is a negative behavioral factor or negative behavioral pattern that is "internal" meaning that it is created from "outside" or "external" oppression that becomes detrimentally individually internalized.

(g.) "Interposition Nullification" a negative behavior very accurately defined by the late well-renowned Track and Field Coach Wilbur Ross as the overall descriptor for the negative human behavior that concerns the physical "oppositional" human behavior as "manifested oppression operationalized through external antisocial competition".

(h.) "Crab(s) in the Bucket Syndrome" a very detrimental "syndrome" (or "a group of negative symptoms that occur together") defined by the author as mutually destructive behavior exemplified in the so called well known "crab mentality" (Wilder, 2015). The author defines this here as negatively occurring symptomatic self and other-destructive behavior that is best represented by the more historically common phrase in the black community, "crabs in a bucket" (directly referring to how captured crabs will pull each other down rather than let any of them escape to the mutual destruction of them all).

What is Neuropyschosocial Concept of Trichotomous "Trinegation"?

"Trichotomous Triple Negativity" or more simply "Trinegation" is composed of three negative human behavioral patterns as three negative factors. They are: internal oppression (represented by "[*int*] *opp + intpos null + crb buc syn*"); Interposition nullification (represented by "[*int*] *opp + intpos null + crb buc syn*"); and car in the bucket syndrome (represented by "[*int*] *opp + intpos null + crb buc syn*"). Together the three factors summarized together create a summative "Trinegative" or the "Trinegative Operation" also known as "Trinegation" (or a negative + a negative + a negative = a "Tri-Summative Negative" or "{[–] + [–] + [–]} = "Trinegative" = [Triple –] or Triple Negative") and their negative arithmetically combined relationship can be illustrated in the following model:

$$[int]\ opp + intpos\ null + crb\ buc\ syn$$

"Trinegation".

The aforesaid abbreviated terminology as the explicative definition for operationalized marginalization can be represented in a mathematical summative format as *"Jus –neg val"* is equal to *"$\sum$[int]opp + intpos null + crb buc syn"*. The aforementioned sequential series of definitions in an equation format is then simplified into the following mathematical formula as: "The Transformation from the Definitive Mathematical Description into the Mathematical Equation" = *jus* (as "≡") *–neg val* = "[int]" *opp* + *intpos* (as "∋") *null* (as "ø") + *crb* ("in the" as "⇓") *buc syn*. This then yields the following equation:

jus (as "≡") *–neg val* = "[int]" *opp* + *intpos* (as "∋") *null* (as "ø") + *crb* ("in the" as "⇓") *buc syn*

Which is then simplified into:

The Final Parsimonious Mathematical "Equation for Operationalized Marginalization" [EOM]:

$$-≡ = [in]o + i∋ø + c⇓bs$$

Thus, in terms of identity:

$$-≡ ≡ [in]o + i∋ø + c⇓bs.$$

Where, the elements for the mathematical formula for the Equation for Operationalized Marginalization are as follows:

1.) *"jus –neg val"* which is also equal to "−≡" = The "Psychophysiosocial" manifestation of "Justification through Negative Validation" or "Negative Justification" espoused by the author James E. Osler II, Ed.D.;

2.) *"[int] opp"* = "[in]o" = The "Philopsychosocial" manifestation of "Internalized Oppression" brought to light by Philliph M. Mutisya Ed.D. (circa a series of discussions and lectures on his research, his long-term observations of human behavior, and his experiences in the United States and on the continent of Africa during 2001-19);

3.) *"int pos null"* = "i∋ø" = The "Physiosocial" manifestation of "Interposition Nullification" attributed to and by world-renowned athletic (Track and Field) Coach Wilbur L. Ross (circa comments he made to author during prolonged discussions about life and his experiences in general during 1998-99); and

4.) *"crb buc syn"* = "c⇓bs" = The "physiological" manifestation of "Crabs in the Bucket Syndrome" that is universally recognized in the black community particularly in the United States and now throughout the diaspora historically for many decades (greatly preceding the turn of the century). This terminology has been more broadly defined and universally applied to human social organization (such as politics) as the so called "Crab Mentality" or

"Crabs in the Bucket Mentality" by former United States—State of Virginia Governor Lawrence Douglas Wilder (the first elected African American State Governor) in his 2015 book entitled, "Son of Virginia: A Life in America's Political Arena". This arena holistically describes the outcome of manifested oppression as the oppressed individual's negative desire to bring others down with them into a collective mire of terminal suffering from continual oppression.

Explanation of the Parsimonious Symbols used in the EOM

The EOM is composed of several mathematical symbols used to simplify the behaviors that create negative justification as a symptom of the combined series trifold of negative human behaviors. The arithmetic symbols are defined as follows:

1.) ≡ = The computational symbol for "Justification" which is derived from computing equal justification to set documentation margins;

2.) [in] = The mathematical symbol for "Internalized" which comes from the complier integer abbreviation "int" (without the "t" for "<u>internal</u>");

3.) ∋ = The mathematical symbol for "Position" which is taken from inverse of the set notation "element of" symbol which is also an "inverted" or "reversed" lower-case Greek letter Epsilon or "E";

4.) ∅ = The mathematical symbol for "Nullification" which has its origins from set notation to indicate an empty set; and lastly

5.) ⇓ = The mathematical symbol for "in the"; which literally has its origins from the inverse of the "double arrow symbol used to denote repeated exponentiation.

Transformation of EOM into a Tripositive Behavioral Pattern via Metacognetic Mechanics

The Upright Transformative Function of Metacognetic Mechanics involves the use of a specific "Upright Trigonometric Function of Metacognetic Mechanics" as imputable bridge that inputs the EOM into an operational procedure that inculcates the individual to seek self-awareness; self-growth; and self-sustainability. Through this cathartic process one becomes aware of the liabilities of internalized oppression and begins to liberate one's self by extricating internally from the deliberating cognitive and affective outcomes of past experiences. It is only through this process that one can truly become free of the stains of interposition nullification via positive biblical holistic metaphysical healing to solve the internal damage done by external experiences. This the solution for all types of negative outcomes that come from the EOM through the process of healing that transforms negatives into positives. In this manner, holistic healing takes place one moves from remembrance to forgiveness; from hatred to peace; from marginalization to empowerment; from ignorance into learning; from wildness to self-control; from denial to acceptance; from bitterness to love; and from destruction to growth. The following model simultaneously explains and defines the "Upright Trigonometric Function of Metacognetic Mechanics".

$$[-\!\equiv\; =\; [in]o + i\!\ni\!\varnothing + c\Downarrow bs] \;\rightarrow\; \left[\;\right] \;\rightarrow\; \left[\oplus = [in]^{\underline{emp}} + \text{Ȣ}^{\underline{enc}} + \Uparrow^{\underline{PGV}}\right].$$

The total outcome of the "Upright Trigonometric Function of Metacognetic Mechanics" or "UTFMM" which is the solution to the EOM is presented in the aforementioned model as:

$$\left[\oplus = [in]^{\underline{emp}} + \text{Ȣ}^{\underline{enc}} + \Uparrow^{\underline{PGV}}\right].$$

This mathematical model is definitively defined as,

1.) $\oplus$ = The Biblical symbol for the ***"Risen Saviour [Jesus Christ] from the Cross"***; furthermore the symbol fully indicates a focus on "Jesus Christ"; it is also used in the Visual Arts discipline of Graphic Design as the logistical symbol for the "Visually Established Justification" of two or more transparent graphics overlaid on top of one another vis transparent mediums (such as vellum, clear film; photographic film; video film: acetate sheets; or transparency film) to create a new "Cohesive Visual Whole"; used in this case as the straightforward symbol for a "concentrated focus" (as it also resembles a measuring "target" generally used within a long-distance scope) on the transformation of negative justification into a stabilized form of "Tripositive Internalized Establishment", thus, this symbol also literally means "To Establish" via a wholeheartedly "*Focus on Jesus Christ*";

2.) $[in]^{\underline{emp}}$ = The mathematical symbol for ***"Internalized"*** which comes from the complier integer abbreviation "int" (without the "t" for "internal") symbolizing "Internalized Empowerment" or "*Inwardly Empowered*";

3.) $\text{Ȣ}^{\underline{enc}}$ = The "hourglass" character (symbolic of "time" as the sand in the hourglass has not yet begun to drain from the top into the bottom of the instrument) with the "enc" abbreviation (symbolizing "encouragement") together which = **"Timely Encouragement"** and most of all is a novel universal symbol for "*Hope*"; and

4.) $\Uparrow^{\underline{PGV}}$ = The mathematical symbol for ***"raise to the"***; which literally has its origins from the "upward double arrow symbol used to denote repeated exponentiation, is conjoined with the capitalized "PGV" for ***"Praise Almighty GOD Vigorously"*** literally meaning to ***"praise Almighty GOD with all of your strength, heart, and mind"*** and most of all is a novel universal symbol for ***"Divine Blessings"*** (as is more commonly stated amongst believers: ***"As the Praises Go Up the Blessings Come Down"***). This is supported by the work of P. F. Steenburg. As stated by Steenberg (2001) in "Christ: a solution to suffering in First Peter", he emphatically states the following: *"Christ is presented as a solution to suffering in first Peter. This is achieved by way of three main arguments. Firstly, a new identity is developed of which Christ forms the center. Secondly, the author provides hope, which includes eschatological hope that can be theirs only through Christ. Lastly, Christ is offered as the rational for endurance. His example is presented for the believers to follow. If the readers accepted the new identity in Christ, grasped onto the hope and followed the example of Christ, their suffering would become bearable in the present and be solved in the future."*

Conclusion

The rationale for this narrative was to identify, functionalize, and explain the damaging effects to human interrelationships due to ongoing oppression (that has damaged Black Americans and HBCUs in particular). The paper also provided a solution to negative human behaviors that are often seen as a result of oppression. Parsimonious abbreviations of neuroscientific, social, and physiological terminology were actively used to define and explain in a novel fashion the mathematics in a series of formulae as the outcomes of oppression. Afterwards a solution was provided as an innovative way of explaining how to resolve the earlier presented negative human behaviors. All of the formulae presented are the innovative logical statements presented as new notations, pioneering models, and idealistic operations that explain (in detail) the how and why persons behave the way they do due to oppression. The author both believes and hopes that by identifying and shedding light on this particular topic that now and in the future, we can ultimately resolve the human negative interaction differences that occur in our lives, in our homes, and in our workplaces. In this manner, oppression can be resolved and identified early on so that persons do not suffer and bring harm to others because they too are suffering because of oppression that manifests through negative behavior. Once the behavior is identified the source of the oppression can be dealt with and healing can take place via the "Upright Trigonometric Function of Metacognetic Mechanics" as the ideal solution provided.

References

Osler, J. E. (2010). Visualus™ © Visioneering Volumetrically: The Mathematics of the Innovative Problem–Solving Model of Inventive Instructional Design (1st ed.). Morrisville: Lulu Publications.

Steenberg, P. F. (2001). Christ: a solution to suffering in First Peter. Verbum et Ecclesia, 22(2), 392-400.

Wilder, L. D. (2015). *Son of Virginia: A Life in America's Political Arena.* Rowman & Littlefield.

CHAPTER: 10 — Exploding HBCU Culture Pathology Part Nine: Whatever Happened to Professorial Prestige in the Academy?

—*Whatever Happened to Professorial Prestige in the Academy?*—

Where is the Academic Freedom and the Shared Governance? A Series of Solutions to Begin to Reclaim Academic Professorial Prestige

[From: Mutisya, P. M., Osler, J. E. & Williams, L. D. (2021). Chapter 11: Whatever Happened to Professorial Prestige in the Academy? Where is the Academic Freedom and the Shared Governance? A Series of Solutions to Begin to Reclaim Academic Professorial Prestige. AAERI Academic Freedom Book. AAERI (Association for the Advancement of Educational Research International)]

Philliph M. Mutisya, James E. Osler II & Larry D. Williams.

Conspectus—

This chapter explores and addresses the current status of the **professorship** in higher education. The authors explore how the prestige of the professorship has dwindled and as a result has changed the overall trajectory of the professor as an active and ongoing integral part that is the essential essence of the Academy. The chapter picks up from the research article initially published in the International Journal of Process Education by Mutisya and Osler in 2014 as well as the much sought-after article published by the same two authors in the Journal of Creative Education published in 2013. The 2013 article involved an in-depth analysis on the professorate from a diverse number of currently employed professors. The research ultimately addressed the need for a *"Conceptual Framework for Faculty as Academic Leaders in the Academy"*. This chapter extends the initial research from 2013-14 into an active discourse on current problems facing the professorate and solutions that can be enacted to reclaim the lost prestige and authority that the position of professor once had in higher education.

Keywords: *Academy, Analysis, Conceptual Framework, Development, Dialogue, Higher Education, Leadership, Problem–Solving, Solutions.*

Introduction

The position of *"Professor"* has historically had a high level of respect both inside and outside of higher education. Professors for the most part outside of the academy were and are currently viewed as well-rounded extensively immersed experts in their chosen fields of expertise. They are relied upon to provide subject matter expertise to media, governments, organizations, and industry. The men and women who occupy these positions are backed by years of research cultivated in publications, creativity, entrepreneurship, teaching, grant-writing, and inquiry. The public has always viewed the professor as an outstanding resource with a wealth of insight and knowledge. However, within the once hallowed halls of the University there is a substantive loss of respect and authority for the professorate. Benjamin Ginsberg in his insightful book, "The Fall of the Faculty and the Rise of the All Administrative University and Why It Matters" (2011) points out that:

"From 1975 to 2005, case after case where proportionally, the number of administrators over the past 40 years has been growing far more rapidly than that of faculty members or students".

The proposed solutions in this chapter provide a more reflective analysis of the leadership in the academy as a critique of the phenomenon that has continued to impugn the role and the status of the Professorship. The authors provide an active discourse on the factors that have diminished the role of the professor through the lens of research and critical critique of higher education. This narrative cumulatively reports how universities have evolved and have contributed to the decline and diminishing prestige of the Professorship thereby adversely affecting academic quality, university culture, and long-term higher education leadership. In this chapter we explore and examine the causes of impunity of the prestigious role that was once held by a Professor in the academy and its impact on and in the academy. Specifically, presented is an in-depth interchange immersed in Ginsburg's authoritative and perceptive critique immersed in, "The Fall of the Faculty".

Defining the Overarching Scope of the Problem

In his review of Ginsberg's book researcher Steven Johnson (2012) states the following:

"In his book, The Fall of the Faculty and the Rise of the All-Administrative University and Why it Matters, Ginsberg rants about the expansion of "deanlets" and "deanlings", and how it is affecting universities today. He puts a good case that the downfall of universities lies in expansion of administrators who do not have an academic or client orientation, but rather a managerial orientation. The author proposes that this administrative blight has been occurring for decades and the vast number of "deanlets" and "deanlings" have drawn funds from faculty pursuits and that many times the administrators and staffers lack any real academic backgrounds. Ginsberg is not the first or the only writer to point this out. The quote "The principal structural operating domain of Extension—University and government—is often cited today as prime examples of bureaucracy" comes directly from Patterson (1997)".

The intent of the Framework published in 2013 was to engage faculty in developing more collaborative approaches that would lead to more effective ways to change the inertia that plagues and has a stranglehold on higher education leadership. The proposed published framework was designed as a guide for faculty empowerment on engaging in becoming more proactively involved in leadership decision-making in their institutions as academic leaders. The framework incorporated the Academy of Process Education (PE) mission and philosophy. The PE mission and philosophy are based on five areas that the authors believe provides a good framework of shaping prestigious professorship profile conceptually: *(1.) Self-development, (2.) Learners Development, (3.) Institutional Development, (4.) Intellectual Development, and (5.) Faculty Development (found at www.processeducation.org).*

<u>Researchers Mutisya and Osler state the following regarding the professorate in their 2013 research article that appeared in the Journal of Creative Education</u>, "In reframing the conceptual framework (mindset) that we introduced in 2013, we posited (based upon in-depth analysis of the existing professorate) that the phenomenon that is expressed by Ginsburg is a pandemic that adversely affects the entire gamut of the academy. This is supported by ongoing research. For example: A quote by Matthew Abraham (2016) at the time an Associate Professor of English at the University of Arizona states in his review of Ginsberg's book states:

"That in the contemporary scene, the major goals associated with the values of a traditional liberal arts education have seemingly been sabotaged by career bureaucrats."

Abraham in his review of Ginsberg's book also emphatically says:

"The self-promotion and puffery associated with administrators, the psychobabble promulgated by those Ginsberg derisively labels as "deanlets" and "deanlings"—not to the mention their dutiful and mindless staffers who carry out their tasks by deploying the rhetoric of excellence and diversity, while in reality protecting administrative interests (not to mention the waste, embezzlement, insider trading, and fraud typifying the corporate university), make a mockery of the core academic mission. Within such a situation, to paraphrase the title of Richard E. Miller's brilliant book, it's as if learning is really beside the point."

The Rapid History of the Problem that Exists in the Current Climate of Higher Education

One may ask the rhetorical question regarding the existing culture in the academy, *"Just how in the world did we come to this?"* This is a very good question. It begs the reader to delve deeper into history to find out exactly how the current structure has manifested into the current university infrastructure. Interestingly enough the problem with current academic environment has manifested in roughly two generations (if we consider that a generation is about twenty years). Ginsberg in 2011 wrote a scathing historical review in his article published in the Washington Monthly entitled, ***Administrators Ate My Tuition***". He states the following occurred historically to create the modern university:

"Forty years ago, America's colleges employed more professors than administrators. The efforts of 446,830 professors were supported by 268,952 administrators and staffers. Over the past four decades, though, the number of full-time professors or "full-time equivalents"—that is, slots filled by two or more part-time faculty members whose combined hours equal those of a full-timer—increased slightly more than 50 percent. That percentage is comparable to the growth in student enrollments during the same time period. But the number of administrators and administrative staffers employed by those schools increased by an astonishing 85 percent and 240 percent, respectively. Today, administrators and staffers safely outnumber full-time faculty members on campus. In 2005, colleges and universities employed more than 675,000 fulltime faculty members or full-time equivalents. In the same year, America's colleges and universities employed more than 190,000 individuals classified by the federal government as "executive, administrative and managerial employees." Another 566,405 college and university employees were classified as "other professional." This category includes IT specialists, counselors, auditors, accountants, admissions officers, development officers, alumni relations officials, human resources staffers, editors and writers for school publications, attorneys, and a slew of others. These "other professionals" are not administrators, but they work for the administration and serve as its arms, legs, eyes, ears, and mouthpieces." (page 2 of 9)

Ginsberg's dialog above provides a brief analytical description of how in the last forty years the academy has evolved into a more business-like structure and practice without embracing what author Osler calls in this chapter *"**The Esprit dé Corps of the Professorate**"* (the terms *"Esprit dé Corps"* in this context is directly defined as the common spirit existing in the members of a group and inspiring enthusiasm, devotion, and strong regard for the honor of the group—or in another manner of speaking *"**the overall respect for collegiality and spirit of the professorate**"*) of the university that includes (but is not limited to): collegiality; peer-to peer respect; transparency; and active and ongoing dialog. The lack of this notion has both led and bred to the current "silo-mentality" that plagues the entire academic enterprise as a whole. Therefore, some semblance of a solution must be found before the academy flounders into a mere mockery of what it once was and never becomes in fullness what it could have been.

The Trend Towards the Emphasis on Over Management in Higher Education Based Upon Non-Positive Industry Mid-Managerial Models

Currently higher education follows a business model that takes the worst examples from enterprise and industry. According to Warren Bennis the trend in organizations is to: "over manage and under lead". This is more evident in higher education than in the corporate sector. There is an implicit assumption that student failure is a reflection of professional effectiveness. As a result, the prevalence of certain trends become instantly obvious to the observer. They are:

1.) Prevailing Trend 1—University administration that have instituted structures to strip faculty of control of the curriculum, course content, and pedagogical strategies; and
2.) Prevailing Trend 2—Faculty as a whole have a diminished role in the development of education content, instructional strategies, and curriculum development; yet they are held responsible for student failure, and administrators receive credit for their success.

Therefore, its not surprising that university leadership from the highest ranks seek to continue to add multiple layers of mid-managerial administrators who proactively complete the two abovementioned negative trends.

The Why of Things: "Why are Universities the Way They Are"

If you were to take a random sample of university leaders at the highest level (Chancellors and Presidents in this day and time) and ask them the overriding question of "Why they exist?", the universal response would be as follows: "We exist for the retention and graduation of students and maintaining "their" (meaning their respective institution's) "financial bottom line". It matters little where the sample is taken or if it's a recognized private university that is regarded as "top tier" or a more regional state federally-supported university. The rationale from the leadership at the highest level is the same. In fact, they (for the most part) all have the same answer. This is very apparent as it is written universally in their respective university visions, missions, objectives, and goals. One of the authors of this chapter (Williams) refers to this line of reasoning as a *"false dilemma"* (or what is often more commonly referred to as a *"false dichotomy"*). In a nutshell, this common mode of thought is an example of an "informal fallacy". Holistically well-defined as a more specific statement that falsely claims itself as an either/or option, when in actuality, there are many other possibilities. The same question posed to a random sample of university scholars would probably get a different response. Such as this: "Why does the university exist?" the scholar would emphatically and passionately state:

"We exist for the sole purpose of educating effective leaders to prepare students with the skills and abilities to meet the need for a changing global environment".

Unfortunately, to the detriment of the faculty and the enterprise in which they serve the university in which they are employed more often takes the stance that their options are mutually exclusive, thus, reinforcing the belief that they should actively and directly thin the ranks of senior faculty and fill the gap with administrators, non-tenured faculty, and adjuncts. Sadly, the decisions to start with the "how" and the "what" instead of the "why of things" empowers the industry example of the mid-management administrative style to stifle and control the professorship. In philosophy, a "formal fallacy" or "non sequitur" (if the premises are incorrect), then the conclusions that come out of such a rationale and reasoning are also flawed. This is the why and how the university is in the position that it is in now. How we proceed forward will determine how the academic enterprise will survive and move forward for generations to come.

Now that the problem has been clearly identified, solutions can now be applied to provide a bountiful and soothing salve to the much-wounded professorship. Indeed, proactive and dynamic solutions are readily available and much needed that can correct the "inertia of the academy". This both and a phrase and a terminology used to describe the current morose in the academy as identified by Osler and Mutisya in their popular 2013 publication, "*A Tri-Squared Analysis to Establish the Need for a Statistical Framework for K–20 Faculty as Academic Leaders*". The aforementioned solutions appear in a step-by-step fashion in the remainder of the chapter.

The Solutions to the Problem Expressed in Steps One and Two

Step One: Exposure of the Problem to Invested Stakeholders Outside of the Academic Arena

It has often been observed that faculty who struggle to survive in the auspices in the modern university may try to influence university via planning and policy-making in a positive manner only to meet with administrative gridlock. This in turn leads to faculty anger and frustration. Professors in this arena quickly find that the university culture sabotages their best efforts. This is best illustrated by an emphatic quote by Chand in 2010. Samuel Chand (2010) states in his powerful and insightful book "Cracking Your Church's Culture Code: Seven Keys to Unleashing Vision and Inspiration" the following: "*Culture Trumps Vision*". Thus, faculty must be aware of the detriment to the prestige of the professorship and the undermining of their authority. University professors must be aware of their internal university influence. Philliph Masila Mutisya defines this best in his phrase that clearly describes and defines faculty university expertise as: "*Custodians of the Curriculum*." Thus, it is incumbent upon the professorate caught in the struggle with the university administration to expose to the greater public exactly what is transpiring in the halls of the academy. As Matthew Abraham stated in 2016:

"It is crucial that faculty publicize administrative malfeasance within their universities. Given that there is increasing interest in the kinds of anecdotal evidence Ginsberg provides in The Fall of the Faculty about administrative abuse, especially in the wake of the 2008 financial collapse, publicizing administrative misdeeds may lead to the gathering of a critical mass of faculty,

students, parents, and alumni who will be prepared to fight back against the theft of the university. Parents will certainly be interested in the kinds of abuses Ginsberg examines, since they are the ones often footing the skyrocketing price of tuition. The next time a student or parent blames escalating tuition bills on increasing faculty salaries, we should be quick to correct them. We should immediately spotlight the salaries of our university's mid- and upper-level managers. Indeed, administrative salaries have not been subjected to the kind of scrutiny they deserve because most people do not know about them, preferring to focus on faculty indolence and self-indulgence. In brief, faculty are convenient scapegoats, absorbing the blame for the effects of administrative expansion and recklessness." (Page 11 of 14)

This clearly illustrates the trichotomous negative attacks on faculty that manifest as: aggression; suppression; and oppression of faculty individual rights by administrators. Thus, faculty fail to emphasize the basic economics of their value to the university. For example, high faculty workloads that equates to exceptional number of students taught per course hours which equates to a high yield in terms of credit per hour value at standardized course cost. At the same time the middle managerial business structure is mired in the suppression of faculty in terms of opportunities to travel, resources, and opportunities to pursue innovation in academic programs. This is made worse in that the very middle management that suppresses the professorate should practice collegiality. In terms of academic credentials via terminal degrees it is level across the university despite titles. Yet it is the very titles that accrue mid-managerial administrative bullying at the expense of faculty collegiality. Unfortunately, this creates a different kind of upward mobility in the academy. The pursuit of titles replaces the required academic trifold expertise of teaching, research, and service as a threshold. This is due to simple equation, "**Titles = Money + Authority**". Considering the current state of affairs in higher education why wouldn't a junior or senior faculty member join the chase for titles rather than be relegated to the ongoing abuse they have experienced within the faculty ranks? Unfortunately, by doing this they themselves become complicit in continuing the ongoing problem. They become the new mid-managerial administrator capable of abusing fellow faculty. This remains true until there is an "academic fall from grace" and the said once powerful administrator has lost their once self-heralded position of administrative power and must return to the ranks of the faculty (provided they have tenure and rank in their respective field). Now collegiality is expected by this individual where they may have been abusive to fellow faculty in their previous administrative position. It makes for an uncomfortable academic environment (to say the least) on both sides of the equation (by both the former administrator and their fellow colleagues). However, it is fortunate that often the past is typically forgotten as they now too have to navigate in this "new normal" often feeling the consequences of having to deal with the ever-present mid-managerial higher education academic environment. This indeed is a very dangerous and untenable situation for the faculty who fall prey to the "Titles = Money + Authority" equation. Step Two follows and provides details on proactive solutions to the existing mire that exists between mid-managerial higher education administrators and faculty.

Step Two: _Proactive Rather than Reactive Solutions to Academic Mid-Managerial Gridlock_

Rather than be punitive an altogether different direction needs to be pursued in the university-setting to heal the rift between administration and faculty. Once the problem has been identified cultural change must take place. Equity and true shared governance must take place rather than aggressive means of suppression. Positions of leadership will still be respected but in turn a "servant-leadership model must become the norm. Mindsets need to change on both sides by both faculty and administrators. The university is "an industry of ideas" and if ideas do not flow then the university as a whole stagnates and ultimately dies. In terms of a change in mindset the research by Carol Dweck meets that very need. Dweck posits that there are two mindsets, one of "Fixed" and one of "Growth". Dweck explains how her observations of children demonstrate that a person's mindset can profoundly influence behavior. She has discovered that people with fixed mindsets believe that their achievements are based on innate abilities. As a result, they are reluctant to take on challenges. People with growth mindsets believe that they can learn, change, and develop needed skills. They are better equipped to handle inevitable setbacks, and know that hard work can help them accomplish their goals. (Dweck, 2008). Dweck in 2006 asserted that Higher education has shifted from the original intent of the academy that was driven by faculty with a focus of creating and developing industry of ideas, and conceptualizing academics as leaders (not administrators or middle managers of people), a shift away from linear business model (institutions) that involves the dynamics of elitist view of academic enterprise that stifles creativity and growth due to the nature of Fixed Mindset as postulated. Stephen Childs supports Dweck's observations in his 2019 article in Forbes that states,

"Stanford University psychology professor Carol Dweck has researched the growth mindset and believes it has significant effects for those leaders who embrace the philosophy. Her findings illustrate that when management promotes a growth mindset among team members, they encourage learning, development and new ideas."

How do we mediate and mitigate **"the unconfirmed academic civil war"** that exists between mid-managerial administrators and the professorate? It is an intriguing question. Obviously both sides of the equation need to co-exist. The middle managerial administrator appears to be _"the new norm"_ in higher education and the university does not exist without the professor. Both sides are going nowhere. Their very existence however it would seem produces the conflict. Is there a way to reduce this? Is conflict resolution between the two sides even possible? Yet another intriguing question. Dweck & Ehrlinger (2006) offer a solution:

"A reluctance to revise impressions of others, once formed, makes conflict resolution particularly difficult because misunderstanding the other plays such a great role in inspiring and exacerbating conflict. This is why those who seek to reduce conflict strive to bring members of both sides together, to educate each side about the others' cultures and histories, and to combat stereotypes and prejudice between groups. As Moshe Davan said, "If you want to make peace, you don't talk to your friends. You talk to your enemies." Through this process, mistaken *impressions are often dissolved and each party gains a better understanding of the other side's perspective."*

There are practical tools that can aid in conflict mediation that are readily available to the academic enterprise. In this chapter we list them as follows:

- Paulo Freire's: Critical Approach to Dialogue also known as "Conscientização" (Freire, 1972);
- Jane Vella's: Dialogue Approach as covered in her "The Little Blue Book of Dialogue Education" (Vella, 2018);
- Mutisya & Osler's: Collaboration Model from the Global Comm–Uni–Versity Model © for the 21st Century (Mutisya & Osler, 2019); in addition, the Academy should also consider the following methods and problem-solving strategies—
- An In-Depth Analysis of the Current Status of Institutional Leadership and Crises as described by and grounded in the work of Ginsberg;
- Peer-to-Peer Mentoring;
- Counseling via the fields of Counselor Education, Psychology, Social Work, and Sociology;
- Conflict Resolution Focus Groups;
- Innovative Methods and Novel Models grounded in faculty expertise designed to address any and all problems that can surface within the confines of the academy;
- Service to the Academic Community-Oriented Leadership versus the abusive Mid-Managerial Administrative Leadership Style by establishing a "Growth Mindset Leadership Training Initiative";
- A leadership model that provides for Professional Leadership Development in the areas of Service Leadership in regards to academic Teaching, Research, and Service;
- Shifting the Higher Education Cultural Paradigm – Analyzing the Ongoing Factors that Contribute to Low Faculty Morale;
- Directly Addressing the often implicitly addressed Higher Education Mid-Managerial Administrative Notions of Disrespect stated as "Faculty Know Nothing & Do Nothing";
- Addressing the Higher Education Mid-Managerial Administrative Notion that "Faculty Must be Controlled";
- Universally adopted Conflict Mediation Methods, Programs, and Strategies; and
- Transformational Leadership Methodologies.

Step Three: <u>Ongoing Discussion and Transparency is Absolutely Necessary if Faculty are to be an Active Part of Leadership in Institutions of Higher Learning</u>

Discourse between faculty and administrators must take place if higher education institutions are to survive and prosper. This is especially true of HBCUs where resources are not as diverse or plentiful as they are at larger major institutions. Professorial prestige comes about because of the time and long investment academicians have placed at the forefront of their careers to innovate, publish, and ultimately become leaders in their respective fields. If the institution as a whole does not take advantage of this expertise, then it is crippling itself. Faculty innovation and expertise are the hallmarks of research, instruction, and funding.

Now more than ever institutions must take time to plan and in into active dialogue with faculty to preserve and reserve their impact, relevance, and unique appeal.

Conclusion & Summary

In this chapter we attempt to enhance and empower professorial prestige by applying a critique of the traditional practice of higher education leadership as perceived by other scholars and through the lens the findings from the initial (and ongoing) analysis that we conducted in 2013-14 to provide more in-depth recommendations and solutions to higher education academic gridlock. The twenty-first century has ushered in an *"academically-stifled era"* where a new breed of higher education administrators has co-opted and curtailed professorial authority and influence. It's a trend that had its genesis in the twentieth century but saw exponential growth fueled by the commercialization of higher education. Caught in the confluence of demographic and structural changes, university administrations shift its focus from an enhanced intellectual climate to one that is an acquiescing to an abusive mid-managerial administrative-style from negative corporate models that has stifled the very nature and ongoing growth of the university in terms of innovative intellectual capacity. In response to these pressures, many universities instituted bloated and complicated administrative infrastructure layers that in almost every aspect of university life have subverted professorial autonomy and authority. This seismic shift in the traditional cultural university milieus has contributed to and produced a cadre of high-paid administrators that instituted have draconian micro-management policies and measures to further erode professorial expertise and pedagogical effectiveness.

Addressing Current and Future Higher Education Leadership with Immediacy and a Sense of Urgency: The Management/Leadership Continuum

A search of the relevant research literature in regards to leadership indicates that there are more than fifteen hundred definitions. Unfortunately, many of the definitions suggest that management and leadership are inextricably intertwined for the sake of simplicity and conceptually clarity. There are clear distinctions between leadership and management. They are not the same. Management prioritizes numbers, is obsessed with surveys, dictates the managing resources, balancing accounting ledgers, establishing supply chain networks, and create spreadsheets, (as stated by Wheatley, 2006). In general, people require direct. Experts with extensive years of knowledge do not need to be managed—they have to be led. Unlike management, "leadership is an art". It is an art that evolves overtime, and is not learned by simply earning pedigrees at prestigious universities, or voraciously consuming leadership literature. It is fundamentally and foremost a practice and one that is ostensive requiring long-term cultivation and practice. *"The leadership journey is not pursued, but ensued; it is a spiritual journey fashioned from personal vicissitudes, challenges, disappointments, psychic pain, and suffering in the trenches of life."* Leadership according to Covey (1990, 2006 & 2013):

"It's an inside out revolution where a character ethic adheres to the principle of personal integrity and the golden rule. It's a departure from the personality ethic that is rooted manipulation, deception, and reputation subjugate honesty, integrity, and fairness."

So, where do we go from here? In this chapter we offered an analysis of the existing problem that adversely affects the prestige of the professorship in the academy. Solutions are provided and listed so that they can be implemented and explored. The start begins with a conversation, albeit a "dialogue". As leadership in higher education begins to change with the conversation and implemented methods of change the prestige of the professorate will immediately reemerge with the corresponding change in the academic climate. The volatility between the faculty and administration will diminish as the dialogue increases because as Jane Vella states, *"The Means to Education is Dialogue and the End of Dialogue is Learning, however, the Purpose Educating is Peace"* (Vella, 2018).

References

Abraham, M. (2016). Review: Benjamin Ginsberg, The Fall of the Faculty: The Rise of the All

Administrative University. Baltimore: Johns Hopkins University Press 2013. Logos: A Journal of
Modern Society and Culture. Accessed on April 13, 2019 at: *https://portside.org/2016-03-30/fall-faculty-rise-all-administrative-university* and also located at: *http://logosjournal.com/2016/abraham-2/*.

Campbell, J. (1949). *The hero with a thousand faces.* New York Books.

Chand, S. R. (2010). *Cracking your church's culture code: Seven keys to unleashing vision and inspiration* (Vol. 54). John Wiley & Sons.

Childs, S. (2019). Why a growth mindset should be a part of your overall business strategy. *Forbes. Forbes Membership Council.* Retrieved from: https://www.forbes.com/sites/forbeshumanresourcescouncil/2019/09/16/why-a-growth-mindset-should-be-a-part-of-your-overall-business-strategy/#59fb06846a8a.

Covey, S. (1990). *The seven habits of highly effective people: Powerful lessons in personal change.* New York: Simon & Schuster.

Covey, S. (2006 & 2013). *The seven habits of highly effective people: Powerful lessons in personal change.* Free Press.

Depree, M. (1989). *Leadership is an art.* New York: A Dell Trademark.

Dweck, C. S. (2006). *Mindset: The New Psychology of Success.* New York: Ballantine Books.

Dweck, C. S., & Ehrlinger, J. (2006). Implicit theories and conflict resolution. *The handbook of conflict resolution: Theory and practice, 2,* 317-330.

Dweck, C. S. (2008). *Mindset: The new psychology of success.* Random House Digital, Inc.

Dweck, C. (2008). Developing a growth mindset. *Highlights Parents. com Interview* http://www. highlightsparents.com/parenting_perspectives/interview_with_dr_carol_dweckdeveloping_a_ growth_mindset. html.

Freire, P. (1972). Pedagogy of the Oppressed. 1968. *Trans. Myra Bergman Ramos. New York: Herder.*

Ginsberg, B. (2011). *The fall of the faculty.* Oxford University Press.

Ginsberg, B. (2011). Administrators ate my tuition. *Washington Monthly, 43*(9-10), 49-56.

Johnson, S. B. (2012). The fall of the faculty and the rise of the all administrative university and why it matters: A book review. *The Journal of Extension, 50* (5), www.joe.org.

Mutisya, P. M., Osler, J. E., Bitting, P. F. & Rotich, J. P. (2014). The Need for a Conceptual Framework for Leadership and Shared Governance between Faculty and Administrators. *The International Journal of Process Education, 6* (1), pp. 43–52.

Mutisya, P. M. & Osler, J. E. (2019). *The Global Comm–Uni–Versity Model © for the 21st century and beyond* (1st ed.) E-Book. OSI © in partnership with Morrisville, NC: Lulu Publications.

Mutisya, P. M., Osler, J. E. & Williams, L. D. (2021). Chapter 11: Whatever Happened to Professorial Prestige in the Academy? Where is the Academic Freedom and the Shared Governance? A Series of Solutions to Begin to Reclaim Academic Professorial Prestige. AAERI Academic Freedom Book. AAERI (Association for the Advancement of Educational Research International).

Osler, J. E. & Mutisya, P. M. (2013). A Tri–Squared Analysis to Establish the Need for a Statistical Framework for K–20 Faculty as Academic Leaders. Special Edition: "Instructional Technique and Technologies". *August Journal of Creative Education (Special Issue on Instructional Technique and Technologies), 4* (8A), pp. 12–18.

Vella J. (2018). *The little blue book of dialogue education: The essentials.* Lambert Academic Publishing.

Wheatley, M. (2006). *Leadership and the new science: Discovering order in a chaotic world.* San Francisco: Beret-Koehler Publishers, Inc.

The Role of Faculties as Academic Leaders:
Towards a Conceptual Framework

(Originally Published in 2014 as—Mutisya, P. M., Osler, J. E., Bitting, P. F., & Rotich, J. P. (2014). The need for a conceptual framework for leadership and shared governance between faculty and administrators. *The International Journal of Process Education*, 6(1), 43-52.)

Philliph M. Mutisya, James E. Osler II, Paul F. Bitting, & Jerono P. Rotich

Conspectus—

The narrative in this Chapter involves an active discourse on ongoing research that points towards the need for a Conceptual Framework for Faculty as Academic Leaders that was originally published in 2014 International Journal of Process Education. The aim of this paper is to propose a Conceptual Framework that would lead to increased faculty awareness, shared governance, and motivation for faculty as leaders in higher education. The intent of the Framework is to engage faculty in developing more collaborative approaches that will lead to more effective ways to change the inertia that plagues and has a stranglehold on higher education leadership. The proposed framework is designed as a guide for faculty empowerment on engaging in becoming more proactively involved in leadership decision-making in their institutions. The framework incorporates the Process Education (PE) mission and philosophy. The PE mission and philosophy are based on five areas: (1) Self-development, (2) Learners Development, (3) Institutional Development, (4) Intellectual Development, and (5) Faculty Development (www.processeducation.org). The Conceptual Framework will provide a new perspective on defining academic leadership. The Tri-Squared Statistic is introduced in this paper as a future tool that will be used to analyze and determine the validity and reliability of the instrument in future studies.

Keywords: Academia, Attitudes, Conceptual Framework, Development, Leadership, Centers, Models, Perceptions, Professional Development, Problem–Solving, Tri–Squared

Introduction

To date university faculty and administrators are struggling to negotiate the balance of power as they face the dynamic challenges brought on by the changes taking place in higher education in the 21st Century. The challenges and changes require a reconceptualization of leadership in the academy. The new conceptualization requires a reflection on today's era. Currently, institutions are required to demonstrate learner knowledge, skills, and dispositions as a part of institutional assessment. Thus, the reconceptualization process needs a coherent Conceptual Framework to serve as a guide towards more effective leadership that is in decline in the academe at the local, national, and globally. The aim of this paper was to explore dimensions and concepts to facilitate the creation and development of a Conceptual Framework that would lead to an increased awareness and motivation as empowerment to faculty in higher education. There is a need for a framework that helps faculty as leaders who have the intent to work collaboratively on developing effective ways of meeting the leadership inertia that has continued to challenge leadership in higher education institutions.

Longitudinal Foundational Research

The initial research investigation in this paper included an examination of experiential observations made over time (starting in 2008). The experimental observations took place during new faculty orientations (at North Carolina Central University (NCCU) from 2009–12); at professional conferences (during the APE Annual Conferences of 2009 and 2012), during the Association for the Advancement of Education Research (AAER) Annual Conference of 2010. Other observations took place in various institutions (including NCCU, Maryland Eastern Shore State University, Florida Agricultural and Mechanical University, and Kenyatta University in Kenya, African during the same time frame). Also, previous observation occurred during Faculty professional development training for more than 5 years led to this longitudinal study. The longitudinal study concluded with an analysis of data collected to explore how faculty perceive their roles as leaders in their disciplines and how they perceive the administration in their respective institutions. An instrument was developed and deployed as a pilot study to collect data that was analyzed as a foundation on determining the dimensions and strategies that would constitute a larger sample. The larger sample will be used to collect data that would lead to testing for reliability and validity of the instrument that would lead to development of the comprehensive Conceptual Framework for faculty as Academic Leaders.

Continuation of the Foundational Research

The data analysis used in this paper is based on the pilot study that was conducted as part of an ongoing research designed to explore how to re-conceptualize the proposed framework for academic leaders in higher education. The research was also designed to guide faculty towards the path towards becoming Academic Leaders. To initiate this effort the author's, propose an "Ongoing Academic Leadership Conceptual Framework". The purpose of this Framework is to provide a dynamic and engaging solutions that involves education professionals communicating and engaging one other to address and solve institutional problems (thereby safeguarding Academic Freedom through Shared Governance). An added outcome of the Ongoing Academic Leadership Conceptual Framework is to empower faculty by having them become leaders in higher education through their freedom to explore and guide institutional enterprise via innovation and social capital.

Identification of the Problem Area

Importance of academic freedom and shared governance is illustrated in a statement by the Higher Education Program and Policy Council. This statement captures the views embraced by most intuitions as far as academic freedom is concerned, it states:

"The concept of academic freedom is based on the idea that the free exchange of ideas on campus is essential to good education. Specifically, academic freedom is the right of faculty members, acting both as individuals and as a collective, to determine without outside interference: (1) the college curriculum; (2) course content; (3) teaching; (4) student evaluation; and (5) the conduct of scholarly inquiry. These rights are supported by two institutional practices shared governance and tenure (see below.) Academic freedom ensures that colleges and universities are "safe havens" for inquiry, places where students and scholars can challenge the conventional wisdom of any field—art, science, politics or others." (p.1)
From: http://www.aft.org/issues/highered/acadfreedom/index.cfm

Further support for the aforementioned statement by the Higher Education Program and Policy Council is supported by an account from the report entitled, "Academic Freedom Under Attack: AMERICAN FEDERATION OF TEACHERS (AFT) – Accountability in Higher Education" (March 2000) that addressed academic freedom by stating:

"Academic freedom rights are under constant attack and because a majority of today's instructors—those in temporary contingent jobs do not have the critical protections these rights provide to the educational process".

In this same report it is further asserted that,

"Academic freedom and its attendant rights do not mean "anything goes." No one would argue that a professor can hold students to his or her belief that the sun revolves around the earth, for example. Faculty must act professionally in their scholarly research, their teaching, and their interactions with students and other faculty. Institutions of higher education and academic disciplines ensure this through policies and procedures that safeguard both students and the academic integrity of the institutions and disciplines."

This same section of the report includes a definition of Shared Governance. This definition that reflects the values intended for the practice of Shared Governance in the majority of most institutions of higher education in the following statement:

"Shared governance is the set of practices under which college faculty and some staff members participate in significant decisions about the operation of their institutions. Shared governance practices differ from campus to campus, but typically the work of shared governance is undertaken by elected faculty committees working with the administration. On AFT campuses, the union contract often guarantees shared governance rights, and the union may play a role in implementing shared governance. Shared governance is democracy in action, intended to ensure that academic decisions are made for strictly academic—not political, commercial or bureaucratic reasons." (p. 1)

The AFT report asserts that,

"Accountability is very important because usually the individual accountability in a shared governance process at the institution level, attention usually centers on the full-time tenured faculty. And these discussions, in turn, usually begin with an understanding (or misunderstanding) of the rights and responsibilities of faculty tenure. To put it simply: Far from being an anachronism, a problem that needs fixing or an impediment to accountability, the tenure system is, in fact, the cornerstone of accountability and institutional excellence." (p.1)

To address the above stated issues, the researchers decided to select a research-based methodology to apply in determining the dimensions that would apply in re-conceptualizing the best approach and the process that would constitute a conceptual framework as a guide for faculty as academic leaders. The fundamental idea was to have a careful and critical movement directed towards relieving faculty and administrators from a pathological blame approach into a sustainable way of engaging faculty in a dialogue and pedagogy that is supported by research. Thus, the research is designed to identify specific problems that would be part of a dialogue to instill social justice, an overall sense of empowerment, and an environment of equity with values grounded in responsibility and accountability.

Rationale for the Research Statistic and Associated Research Methodology

The Tri–Squared Statistical model was used to analyze data to determine the attitudes and perceptions of faculty as leaders. Many statistical measures used in education are based on experimental research designs that require scientific methodologies and cannot be implemented in educational institutions without violating legal policies or severely disturbing the learning environment associated instructional climate. To promote the previously mentioned efforts towards empowering faculty in the areas of social justice, empowerment, and environmental equity novel statistical measures and methods are required that are specifically designed for education and educational environmental needs. The Tri-Squared statistical model provides scientific subsequent measures based on rigor and grounded in the foundation of longstanding educational research, fundamental educational theory, and innovations in qualitative, quantitative, and mixed methods research designs native to the specifics of pedagogy and andragogy (Osler, 2012).

The Total Transformative Trichotomous–Squared Test provides a methodology for the transformation of the outcomes from qualitative research into measurable quantitative values that are used to evaluate the validity of hypotheses. The advantage of this statistical model is in its design which is a comprehensive holistic testing methodology and consistent in holistically measuring categorical variables relevant to educational and social behavioral environments, where the established methods of pure experimental designs that can be violated easily. The unchanging base of the Tri–Squared Test is the 3 × 3 Table based on Trichotomous Categorical Variables and Trichotomous Outcome Variables. The emphasis on the three distinctive variables provides a thorough rigorous robustness to the test that yields enough outcomes to determine if differences truly exist in the environment in which the research takes place. The Tri–Squared analysis procedure uses an innovative series of mathematical formulae that do the following as a comprehensive whole: (1) Convert qualitative data into quantitative data; (2) Analyze inputted Trichotomous qualitative outcomes; (3) Transform inputted Trichotomous qualitative outcomes into outputted quantitative outcomes; and (4) Create a standalone distribution for the analysis on possible outcomes and to establish an effective research effect size and sample associated alpha level to test the validity of an established research hypothesis (Osler, 2012).

The Tri–Squared Test Research Design Methodology

The Tri–Squared Research Design Methodology as Used in this Study is as follows:

Step One: Design of an Inventive Investigative Instrument that has Trichotomous Categorical Variables and Trichotomous Outcome Variables.

Step Two: Establish the Research Effect Size, Sample Size with associated Alpha Level.

Step Three: Establish Mathematical Hypotheses.

Step Four: Use the Tri–Squared Test as the Data Analysis Procedure following Implementation of the Investigative Instrument. This is the final step in the Tri–Squared Test. An example of the research design reporting methodology follows in the Standard Tri–Squared 3 × 3 Tabular Format on the page that follows.

The Research Hypotheses

Mathematical Hypotheses:

$$H_0: Tri^2 = 0$$
$$H_1: Tri^2 \neq 0$$

Results of the Tri-Squared Test

A pilot study data was aggregated and analyzed using the Tri–Squared Statistic to determine faculty responses to the proposed Conceptual Framework. The major areas of foci ware the importance of how higher education faculties perceive and exercise their academic freedom from an empowerment aspect in the spirit of shared governance. The study is intended to provide a knowledge table to help in further "revisioning" and "remodeling" of the Conceptual Framework as a guide for faculty as academic leaders. Ultimately, the Conceptual Framework is intended to empower faculty and reinforce shared governance and academic freedom.

Table One

Conceptual Framework for Faculty as Academic Leaders Tri-Squared Test

Reported below is a sample Tracheotomy–Squared Test illustrating the standard 3 × 3 Tri–Squared Formula and qualitative table of outcomes reporting results using the standard Tri–Squared 3 × 3 Format. Sample data analyzed using the Trichotomous T–Square Three by Three Table was designed to analyze the research questions from an Inventive Investigative Instrument with the following Trichotomous Categorical Variables: a_1 = Level of Collegiality [Items: A1–A8]; a_2 = Ability to Influence Policy [Items: B1–B6]; and a_3 = Overall Communication of Relevant Information [Items: C1–C10]. The 3 × 3 Table has the following Trichotomous Outcome Variables: b_1 = Agree; b_2 = Disagree; and b_3 = No Opinion. The Inputted Qualitative Outcomes were reported as follows:

$n_{Tri} = 25$

$\alpha = 0.975$

TRICHOTOMOUS CATEGORICAL VARIABLES

	a_1	a_2	a_3
b_1	3	13	12
b_2	20	10	11
b_3	2	2	2

TRICHOTOMOUS OUTCOME VARIABLES

$$Tri^2\ d.f. = [C-1][R-1] = [3-1][3-1] = 4 = Tri^2_{[\bar{x}]}$$

The Tri–Square Test Formula for the Transformation of Trichotomous Qualitative Outcomes into Trichotomous Quantitative Outcomes to Determine the Validity of the Research Hypothesis:

$$Tri^2 = T_{Sum}\ [(Tri_x - Tri_y)^2 : Tri_y]$$

Tri^2 Critical Value Table = 0.484 (with $d.f.$ = 4 at α = 0.975). For $d.f.$ = 4, the Critical Value for p > 0.975 is 0.484. The Calculated Tri–Square Value is 10.939, thus, the null hypothesis (H_0) is rejected by virtue of the hypothesis test which yields the following: Tri–Squared Critical Value of 0.484 < 10.939 the Calculated Tri–Squared Value.

Summary of Table One: Table One illustrates the qualitative transformation into quantitative data as a mathematical application of the Trichotomous–Squared ("Trichotomy–Squared", "Tri–Squared" or "Tri–Square") statistical analysis procedure on a Conceptual Framework for Faculty. Table One shows that participants primarily and overwhelmingly selected the "Disagree" Categorical Variable (a_1b_2 = 20) in terms of Collegiality. In addition, all Categorical Variables were reported respectively as: Level of Collegiality as "Agree" (a_1b_1 = 3), "Disagree" (a_1b_2 = 20), and "No Opinion" (a_1b_3 = 2); Ability to Influence Policy as "Agree" (a_2b_1 = 13), "Disagree" (a_2b_2 = 10), and "No Opinion" (a_2b_3 = 2); and Overall Communication of Relevant Information as "Agree" (a_3b_1 = 12), "Disagree" (a_3b_2 = 11), and "No Opinion" (a_3b_3 = 2). The mathematical formula for the Tri–Squared was reported illustrating the final outcome of the research hypothesis test: the null hypothesis (H_0) is rejected at p > 0.975 is 0.484 (Osler, 2012). Thus, this illustrates that there is a need for a Conceptual Framework for shared governance in higher education to address the deficits in collegiality, policy, and communication between faculty and leadership. Furthermore, more in–depth research is needed to determine foci areas and the extent to which the areas in this study identify as concerns are reflected with a broader audience to better implement the Process Education Conceptual Framework model presented in this study.

A Solution: The Process Education Model as an Ideal Conceptual Framework for Faculty as Academic Leaders

In the search for an ideal Conceptual Framework to address issues concerning Academic Freedom and Shared Governance the questions were designed to create variables based on Process Education Model. Process Education conceptual guiding principles centered on: self–development, learner development, knowledge construction, institutional development, professional development, and teaching/learning in the academy. Process Education Compass (forthwith referred to as "PE") provided the dimensions used in designing the research questions designed to investigate the issues and concerns raised by faculty during the observation period and also from the literature.

The Proposed Conceptual Framework is grounded in suggested strategies that incorporate an integrated approach that includes: critical view on theory and practice, (self–reflection) examining the role of reflection in teaching and philosophical orientation as an applied methodology, and a means to eradicating contradictions in policies and procedures imposed on the institutional process. As a solution, professional growth and development was assessed through examination of the practitioner's world view that was based on their beliefs as the foundation of their professional philosophy. Philosophy involves the systematic development of theories of knowledge, truth, existence, sameness, cause, and good. It requires a steady and persistent effort to increase our understanding of the world, an understanding that is essential if we are to make the world a better place. The constant in all approaches is change, which requires us to interpret the world to change it, which requires critical or philosophical thought (*Philosophy in Classroom Teaching: Building the gap by David A. Jacobson, 2003*). Jacobsen, 2003) further points out that,

"The growing challenge for teaching today is not the availability of knowledge but the need to examine the knowledge and reflect on it. Thus, philosophical application in classroom requires us to examine the ideas, engage in dialogical inquiry, and respect the humanity of our students. By doing that we will be able to facilitate the practical role of philosophy in the classroom and thus address the need to "do something" which creates an alternative ways of viewing existing information and sharpening learner's ability to process and acquire knowledge."

Morrison (2003) points out, the teachers' beliefs about their ability to teach effectively and about the ability of their students to learn highly correlates with student's achievement. Collective Teacher Efficacy is an emergent group–level attribute and the product of the interactive dynamics of group members (Collegial relationship). The groups "shared belief in its conjoint capabilities to organize and execute courses of actions required to produce given levels of attainment correlates to successful professional development" (P. 5– 8). This aspect applies to faculty teaching in higher education as well. Most faculties with a terminal degree who were not exposed to philosophy and psychology as part of theoretical process in teaching and assessment of learning tent to teach their subjects in the way they were taught. Without professional development opportunities that can help them build the necessary knowledge, skills, and dispositions, leave them struggling with how they survive in the profession. Also, if they are involved in an institution that does not practice leadership with shared governance; they tend to be just observers or spectators on the sidelines of the academic leadership. As a result, the lack of a coherent Conceptual Framework to empower faculty as part of the decision-making in the institution leaves them with little or no professional training leading to lack of professional and self–efficacy.

Bandura (1994) defines perceived self–efficacy as the people's beliefs about their capabilities to produce designated levels of performance that exercise influence over events that affect their lives. Self–efficacy beliefs determine how people feel, think, motivate themselves and behave. Such beliefs produce these diverse effects through four major processes. They include cognitive, motivational, and affective and selection processes (aesthetics). A strong sense of efficacy enhances human accomplishment and personal well–being in many ways. People with high assurance in their capabilities approach difficult tasks as challenges to be mastered rather than as threats to be avoided. However, as Chand (2011) reminds us that,

*"**Culture trumps vision**…"*

According to Chand (2011) Organizational cultures includes tangibles and intangibles– the things we can see are the way people dress and behave, the look of corporate offices (HBCUs' buildings and offices), and messages of posters on the walls. However, the intangibles may be harder to grasp, but they give a better read on the organization's true personality, P.28). He further states that organization's values which whether stated or unstated, beliefs, and assumptions; what and how success is celebrated; how the organization solves problems are addressed; the manifestations of trust and respect at all levels of the organization are the intangible elements of culture, which are sometimes identified and often camouflaged. Faculty has to be part of the process of defining the institution culture in order to take ownership of any change needed for growth and trust in the institutional leadership.

Chand (2011) further points that, many leaders confuse culture with vision and strategy which are very different because vision and strategy focus on products, services, and outcomes. He also asserts that culture is about people and it is the most valuable asset in the organization. This raises a very sore spot according to our observation on HBCUs culture especially that Chand asserts, "the way people are treated, the way they treat their peers, and the way their response to their leaders is the air people breathe" (p. 18). As he puts, it if that air is clean and healthy, people thrive and the organization succeeds– but to the extent that it is toxic, energy subsides, creativity lags, conflicts multiply, and production declines. The authors have observed these experiences especially in HBCUs by witnessing this type of climate, however there are fewer efforts towards addressing the issues, thus resulting to blame games where by the status of "wait and see" prevails. Chand (2011) observed that, institutions with strong and vibrant people do more and try their very best to reach their goals guided by spiritual leaders who invite meaningful participation from every person at all levels of the organization or institution. All participants must work together with a common purpose that is discussed and understood and celebrate each other's accomplishments. In this respect, we have observed that in the institutional culture what is celebrated tends to be the iconic or symbolic in nature (based on "we vs. I") and if one does not know the context, which is rarely expressed but known, may mistake it from fake or empty praise. Greenfield at' al (2010) postulates that:

"Understanding and accounting for the impact of organizational context and culture on "Interprofessional Learning" ("IPL") and "Interprofessional Practice" ("IPP") has been given inadequate attention both by practitioners and scholars. Practitioners often try to engender IPL and IPP without adequately considering the richness or challenges of context (Cott, 1998). Social science investigators can conduct research without adequately considering the impact of the locally shared values, beliefs and behaviors (Alvesson, 2002), and the organizational constraints, the human and physical resources of an institution, broader policy and political environments (Baum, 1997; Shulman, 1997)." (Greenfield at' al, 2010).

Process Education Adoption, Challenges, and Training

Process Education Training was embraced by the faculty and administrators at North Carolina Central University (NCCU) in 2008. The faculty learned Process Education Strategies that included Assessment Rubrics. Training by the Pacific Crest through the NCCU Center for Teaching and Learning ignited an interest that led to the formation of a Process

Education Learning Community to address the challenges that were previously identified during workshops conducted with NCCU faculty over 5 years. Some of the challenges addressed at that time included the difficulties faculty had in teaching 21st Century learners who have come to be known as "digital natives".

The challenges uncovered at NCCU during training are found in other institutions of higher learning. These challenges are addressed in the PE Faculty Training Handbook by Dan Apple (Pacific Crest–Process Education) who asserts that,

"In the 21st century, colleges and universities are called to educate people whose knowledge, abilities, and values will enable our post-modern culture to deal with unprecedented, complex, and rapidly changing issues such as environmental risk, sustainable progress, and globalization".

He goes on to further point out that, innovativeness and accountability by the faculty as well as the student has to become more prevalent. He states that there is also an increased demand via higher expectations that require institutions to meet the needs of students through institutional effectiveness both heightened and influenced by pressure from the accreditation standard movement, (http://www.pcrest.com/efgb4/front/preface.htm#Resource).

The perspective addressed by Apple is also shared by the American Association of Colleges and Universities (AACU). In the AACU Greater Expectations Report they specifically stated:

"Today's economic uncertainties challenge all of us to be creative in meeting our commitments to students. These uncertainties also make even more urgent the need for us to prepare all students to thrive in a turbulent and fluid world. Now, more than ever, members are championing the value of a liberal education for individual students as well as for a nation dependent on economic creativity and democratic vitality. Colleges, universities, state systems and other partners are engaging the public and the academy with core questions about what really matters in college, using new clarity about essential learning outcomes to organize their efforts to pursue educational excellence, assess learning, and align school with college and goals with practices." (Preface, January 20–23, 2010).

A study by Sheftall (2006), observed that, there was little dialogue and understanding on how the faculty share leadership with administrators and as such, there was a disconnect in communication between administrators and faculty in terms of the spirit of Shared Governance. This tends to create an antagonistic relationship between faculty and administrators, which impacts their perception and motivation and their responsibilities as part of the Shared Governance of the institution. Thus, the relationship between faculty and administrators tends to be based on a blame game where faculty blame administrators for what is going wrong and administrators tend to look for faculty to do their part but without blaming the administrators, as pointed by Ginsberg, 2011. These challenges are not unique to the authors' institutions because they have been identified in other institutions as well. This is stated in Preface of the PE Faculty Handbook:

"At institutions across the country, new faculty members are faced with a novel and varied set of professional challenges as they begin their academic careers. They are quickly confronted with responsibilities in areas in which they have little or no expertise. Furthermore, criteria for success are broader and expectations are rising. In this changing world, old models of a successful faculty member are of limited usefulness. The new models incorporate well–defined performance criteria in areas besides traditional teaching, research, and service. The central challenge for faculty is to deeply understand what their institutions expect of them in these new performance areas, and to promote development in the areas that are most critical through the use of an annual professional development process."
(http://www.pcrest.com/efgb4/front/preface.htm#Resource.)

North Carolina Central University (NCCU) Process Education (PE) Learning Community started discussion on solutions to the challenges facing faculty collaborating across disciplines within the University, specifically in the arts and sciences. This aided in the production of much needed skills and dispositions that are advantageous to 21st Century classroom teaching and learning. The uniqueness of the NCCU–PE Model was the primary focus on addressing the immediate problems faced by faculty (especially in classroom settings). Solutions were provided through the use of Process Education strategies. Vitally important was the emphasis on Shared Governance. This empowering culture was created through the teaming of faculty with administrators to solve specifically identified challenges. The methodology for doing this was the framing the process based on the five aspects described in the Process Education Star Model which includes: Self Development, Professional Development, Institutional Development, Learner Development and Intellectual Development.

As a result, the NCCU–PE model expanded from its initial University confines into a University-wide interdisciplinary perspective which was expanded further into an inter-institutional partnership that involved authors from many other institutions. The inter-institutional collaboration also resulted in NCCU gaining institutional membership in the Academy of Process Education. The membership has facilitated a proposal for developing a regional inter–institutional chapter with both international and global collaborative linkages. The linkages are specifically aimed at collaborating with African institutions of higher education and other professional development partners. As result of the NCCU-PE training a PE Faculty Learning Community the idea of developing a conceptual framework to guide faculty professional training was born that led to conducting a pilot study to develop research based approach for developing a process that would serve conceptual guide in the ongoing discourse and research on improving faculty professional development as an empowerment process.

Towards a Conceptual Framework of Academic Freedom and Shared Governance

The authors of this study collaborated to develop an empirical study that explored Faculty Perceptions and Attitudes regarding Academic Freedom and Shared Governance. These two areas defined the main problem that poses most of the challenges for faculty academic leaders. Thus, the pilot study was used to identify the variable for consideration that confirmed the need for a Conceptual Framework for Faculty as Academic Leaders. Richard (1993) defines a Conceptual Framework as "consciously organized arrangements of related information that, because we are aware of them, influence our actions". He further asserts that,

"The degree to which we understand our own Frameworks and the Frameworks of others is often the degree to which we achieve unthreatened and successful human interactions. Our own personal Frameworks are often determined by our cultures and to understand the significance of this observation, we must have an understanding of culture in general because we all view our world thorough culturally influenced Frameworks that often collide with the different Frameworks of others, which creates a conflict and thus we feel threatened."

Faculties in higher education face many challenges that demand changes in the conceptualization of the profession and ways to protect the prestige of professorship within the academy. These challenges are not only experienced locally, but depending on one's location in the world, are experienced both nationally and internationally. While there are many reasons that account for the challenges facing higher education faculty, the main ones are the inevitable changes that take place as we continue to grow and become more interdependent and connected globally. There appears to be an eminent change in the attitudes of those involved in higher education. However, the culture within higher education institutions has stagnated and remains the same. Failure to adapt, communicate, and change has resulted in a diminished prestige of professorship and the academy in general.

Collins and Apple (in EFGB, 1.2.4) have established a comprehensive faculty professional profile. This profile makes an excellent foundation for a Conceptual Framework as a guide to conceptualize professionalism in teaching and learning. They specifically point out that:

"More and more, institutions are looking at clarifying faculty performance using Boyer's model of scholarship as a basis (Boyer, 1997). As the external pressures on institutions of higher education have mounted, the importance of elevating the skills of the professoriate keeps increasing (State Higher Education Executive Officers, 2005). The profile in Table 1 provides u basis for understanding eight dimensions of faculty performance. It is recommended that faculty use the profile to formulate an annual professional development plan; to conduct assessment during the academic year to increase performance; and to document in an annual assessment report successes, growth, and plans for future development."
http://www.pcrest.com/efgb4/front/preface.htm#Resource

We argue that there is a critical need for a Conceptual Framework that faculty can use as a guide in collaborating to combat the challenges that face higher education faculty and leadership today. The Framework must be relevant and has to embrace the academy need on engaging faculty as Academic Leaders in the spirit of Shared Governance which demands addressing the following aspects the foundation on developing a comprehensive framework for faculty as Academic Leaders:

1. *A Needed Paradigm Shift* that is conceptualized to address the changing roles of faculty in higher education in the way professors view themselves and how they are viewed as professionals in their respective disciplines (in terms of being respected as authorities of the spheres that they influence that has impacted the role of the academy negatively and its purpose of preparing a well-rounded citizenry). This condition requires a Conceptual Framework that includes concrete professional development that embraces the 21st Century professorship and its prestige that is divergent in thinking;

2. *Lack of an Active Role in Leadership* and control of the profession by having less say in what professors do as professionals (which is contradictory to the profession) as the professorate is the most esteemed notable recognized in the institution. This recognition is the very fiber of the academic society. It is the professors who guide the institution in its development in terms of: Education, Economics, Social Capital, Political Responsiveness, Social Justice, and a variety of Psychological and Philosophical Perspectives;

3. *Consequences of the Assault on Academic Freedom* that has led to prescriptive/convergent-oppressive teaching and learning conditions. That is toxic, antagonistic, and contradictory. This aspect contradicts the very practice where research is supposed to inform teaching and learning. This is lethal to academics and the process of advocating for equitable policies and procedures that empowers the learner and the professor. In other words, the practice has stagnated and stifled the ability of professors to advocate because they are not doing the talking or on the table when the important and fundamental decisions are made;

4. *Innovativeness has been Protracted* – resulting in the loss of the capacity to combat apathy and thereby maintain empathy and the skills that are imperative in sustaining academic life. This has lead to a pathological dependency on a creative bankruptcy that has stifled resourcefulness by the professorate; and

5. *The Climate in the Academy has also Resulted in a Lack of: "TRRFCC" ("Trust, Respect, Responsibility, Fairness, Caring, and Citizenship")* that are the remedy to the toxic academic mindset. A toxic and ambiguous academic climate that has evolved into a climate that is antagonistic leading to apathy and fear whereby even tenured and Full Professors are intimidated. This in turn, affects the overall intellectual climate and has radically lowered expectations thereby impacting academic achievement. This was evidenced in the study by the lack of participation by faculty at all levels due to the fear of administration repercussions.

As part of the study on the continuous active discourse on developing a Conceptual Framework for faculty as academic leaders, we developed a survey designed to explore the perceptions and attitudes of faculty in higher towards Academic Freedom and shared Governance described as part of the conclusion in this paper. We decided to use the collected data as a pilot study because the population sample was not large enough to test for reliability and validity of the study. The collection of the data was limited by the program that was used and to administer the survey because the participants had difficulties in completing the survey successfully. However, the analysis of the sample data of a population (N-25) gave us some insights of the need for developing a comprehensive Conceptual

Framework as a guide for faculty as academic leaders. More data will be collected with revised survey version that would lead to establishing a comprehensive Conceptual Framework as a guide for faculty that would serve as a guide to empowering faculty in sharing leadership and protecting academic freedom.

Conclusion

This study provided an active discourse on ongoing research that yielded to development of a proposed Conceptual Framework for Faculty as Academic Leaders. The Five concepts of the Process Education Model (Self-assessment, Learner development, Institutional Development, Intellectual Development, and Professional development) are used in conceptualization of the proposed Conceptual Framework for faculty as Academic leader. The analysis of the pilot study suggests there is a need for developing a comprehensive Conceptual Framework for faculty as Academic Leader, and it would lead to an increased awareness and motivation for faculty in higher education. The intent of the Framework is to aid faculty to develop more collaborative approaches that lead to effective ways to break the inertia that plagues leadership and provides a continuous challenge in institutions of higher education. The research methodology used to determine faculty outlook on shared governance and analyzed the data in this study was Tri–Squared Statistical Analysis. The Tri–Squared Test yielded the following results in support for the need for developing a Conceptual Framework for faculty as leaders: Tri^2 Critical Value Table = 0.484 (with *d.f.* = 4 at α = 0.975). For *d.f.* = 4; the Critical Value for p > 0.975 is 0.484; and The Calculated Tri–Square Value was 10.939. Thus, the null hypothesis (H_0) is rejected by virtue of the hypothesis test which yielded the following: Tri–Squared Critical Value of 0.484 < 10.939 the Calculated Tri–Squared Value. As a result of the application of this novel mixed methods data analysis research design evidence was shown that clearly supports the need for developing Conceptual Framework for faculty as leaders that promote shared governance and academic freedom. The researchers plan to continue the investigation with a larger sample to further validate the research outcomes and add a greater level of generalizability to the research findings in the future.

References

Academy of Process Educators: Retrieved November 4, 2012, from: http://www.processeducation.org/.

American Federation of Teachers Aft-Accountability in Higher Education. (2000). Washington, DC: Higher Education Department. Retrieved February, 2013 from: http://www.aft.org/issues/highered/acadfreedom/index.cfm.http://www.greaterexpectations.org/.

Beverly, G.-S. (2006). Shared Governance, Junior Faculty, and HBCUs. Publications & Research Academe.

Boyer, E. L. (1997). Scholarship reconsidered: Priorities of the professoriate. San Francisco: Jossey–Bassin. Retrieved November, 2012 from: http://www.pcrest.com/efgb4/front/preface.htm#Resource

Bransford, J. D., Brown, A. L., & Cocking, R. R. (Eds.). (2000). How People learn: Brain, mind, Experience, and School. Washington, DC: National Academy Press. Retrieved December, 2012 from in http://www.pcrest.com/efgb4/front/preface.htm#Resource.

Bransford, J. D., Brown, A. L., & Cocking, R. R. (Eds.). (2000). *How people learn: Brain, mind, experience, and school.* Washington, DC: National Academy Press in. http://www.pcrest.com/efgb4/front/preface.htm#Resource.

Chand, S. R. (2011). Cracking your Churches Culture Code. San Francisco: Jossey–Bass.

Ginsberg, B. (2011). The fall of the Faculty: The Rise of the All–Administrative University and Why It Matters. New York: Oxford University Press.

Greenfield, D., Nugus, P., Travaglia, J., & Braithwaite, J. (2010). Auditing an organization's interprofessional learning and interprofessional practice: the interprofessional praxis audit framework (IPAF). Journal of interprofessional Care, 24(4) 436-49.

Guy-Sheftall, B. (2006). Shared governance, junior faculty, and HBCUs. *Academe, 92*(6), 30-34.

Leise, C., (2010). Improving Quality of Reflecting on Performance. International Journal of Process Education, 2 (1) 65-75.

Mutisya, P. M., Osler, J. E., Bitting, P. F., & Rotich, J. P. (2014). The need for a conceptual framework for leadership and shared governance between faculty and administrators. *The International Journal of Process Education, 6*(1), 43-52.

Osler, J. E. (2012). Trichotomy–Squared – A Novel Mixed Methods Test and Research Procedure Designed to Analyze, Transform, and Compare Qualitative and Quantitative Data for Education Scientists who are Administrators, Practitioners, Teachers, and Technologists. July–September iManager's International Journal on Mathematics, 1(3)

Richard, B.V. (1993). Developing Intercultural Communication Skills. Malabar: Kriger Publishing Company.

State Higher Education Executive Officers. (2005). *Accountability for better results: A national Imperative for higher education.* Washington, DC: National Commission on Accountability in Higher Education. Retrieved January, 2013 from: http://www.pcrest.com/efgb4/front/preface.htm#Resource.

CHAPTER: 12

Exploding HBCU Culture Pathology Part Eleven: 50 Years of Freire's "Pedagogy of the Oppressed" from a Mentor to a Mentee

A Reflection: 50 Years of Freire's Pedagogy of the Oppressed from a Mentor to a Mentee

Philliph M. Mutisya

Conspectus—

The 2020 COVID-19 Pandemic crises has revealed major catastrophic events and effects that has disconnected the whole world. It is ironic that it has manifested itself on the 50th year of Paulo Freire's seminal book, the "Pedagogy of the Oppressed" (originally published during 1970 and republished in 1994) that originated with Critical theories that was shaped by Freire's critical world view.

I was fortunate to have such a preeminent scholar such as the esteemed Paulo Freire as a visiting Scholar at The University of Massachusetts at Amherst (UMASS) when I was in graduate school. During this time at Amherst I was whereby exposed to his book as one of the core readings in my Master's degree program at the UMASS Center for International Education. The "Pedagogy of the Oppressed" book which Freire had written 30 years ago at that time was coupled by his informative and impacting discussions and lectures in which I was an active participant. Freire's assertion caught my attention regarding how education has been conceptualized from a Western World view that *"All education is with a purpose and that purpose can only be political, for either we educate to liberate or we educate to dominate".* This statement immediately caught my attention because it forced me to start analyzing education from a critical perspective as well as a conceptual process that directly led to enhancing my consciousness and creating a new awareness in my thinking.

Freire engaged us as graduate students and faculty to start valuing Critical Pedagogy from a perspective that involves decoding the so called "Hidden Curriculum" that can also be identified as the "unexpressed perpetuation of dominant culture" that is disseminated through an institutional process that shapes one's world view. Critical Pedagogy therefore involves a deep metacognitive analysis that involves more than just the traditional "3Rs" of reading, writing, and arithmetic.

As a part of the in-depth metacognitive meta-analysis involved in Critical Pedagogy one may determine that there are multiple types of literacies expressed as languages that include the following as identified by Wink. They are:

- Functional – languages of street and life;
- Academic – language of schools and universities;
- Workplace – languages of our jobs;
- Information – languages of technology;
- Constructive – languages we construct with the printed word;
- Emergent – languages constructed with texts before we decode;
- Cultural – language that reflects the perspective of culture; and
- Critical – languages that take us deeper into more complex understanding of the world and word and the world, that provides a foundation reflective of multiple experiences and make sense of our world through reading, writing and reflecting (Wink, 2005).

Freire taught us how to deconstruct "internationalized oppression" from a methodology that he developed while working with peasants in his native country of Brazil. It is a methodology that directly involved Paulo Freire himself as an active participant, and was initially formulated through his work in the slums of Brazil. He began to conceptualize a process of "conscious-raising" leading towards a dynamic concept of liberation and then towards what he refers to as "a more complete humanness". The product of this process he referred to as **"Conscientização".**

Conscientização as whole is defined as, *"a degree of consciousness in which individuals are able to see the social system critically".* *The participants in this conscious-raising methodology are able to understand the resultant contradictions in their own lives, to generalize those contradictions to others around them, and transform society creatively with others.* The process is coded into three levels that are: **"Magical", "Naïve" and "Critical".** Freire's methodologies formed a foundation of Critical Literacy.

Today Conscientização as a methodology has created a necessity for developing a theory as a technology to unpack consciousness through the novel creative science that is known as *"ArtiVisual Intelligence ™ ©"* and the ideology of the acronym called, *"STREAM"*—which stands for: *"Science* (as an academic discipline that covers all areas that in-delve in the study natural phenomena); *Technology* (as an overriding area that covers all fields of endeavor that work tools that enable human being work at easier and greater capacity); *Reading* (the academic area that holistically covers any and all forms of "literacy"); *Engineering* (as an academic discipline that covers problem-solving); *Art* (as the academic discipline and arena of active creation)"; and lastly *Mathematics* (as an academic discipline that is the abstract and symmetrical science that studies numbers as quantities and their applications to change, shapes, structures, and space). Altogether STREAM comprehensively encompassed as *"ArtiVisual Intelligence ™ ©* as novel field of holistic innovative creating and problem-solving.

Brown (1978) in "Literacy in 30 Hours by Paulo Freire" asserts the following regarding literacy in the context of Freire's Conscientização methodology (key emphasis on salient points relevant to the topic are bolded and underlined by the author):

"Learning to read is a political act. In a literate society being able to read is a necessary step toward making decisions and sharing power. A non-literate person may be very powerful within a non-subculture, but within the dominant culture a nonreader literate (sic) is marginal. He/She cannot fill out tests and applications, cannot determine what is in contracts without a trusted adviser who can read, has no access to information controlled by professionals, and often is denied the right to vote. Learning to read gives access to information, protection against fraud, and participation as a citizen."

Learning to read is a-step-toward political participation. *But how people exercise their ability to read reflects in part the political attitudes of their teachers. If non-readers learn to read by writing and reading their own words and opinions, then they learn that their perceptions of reality are valid to others and can influence even those in authority.* **If, on the other hand, their teachers require them to learn the words and ideas in a primer which is donated by those in power, then the learners must accept that experience as more valid than their own. They must accept the concepts of social and economic structure transmitted by the teacher or decide not to learn to read.** By understanding the political dimensions of reading, *Paulo Freire developed materials that enabled adults to learn to read in 30 to 40 hours.* This is indicative of Freire's emphasis and impetus on the deconstruction of the problem by those who are most victimized and marginalized. As Freire most famously stated, *"All education is with a purpose and that purpose can only be* *political, for either we educate to liberate or we educate to dominate"* ~ *Paulo Freire* **(1994).**

The Conscientização methodology and concepts were operationalized by (Smith, 1975) in his UMASS dissertation that established the coding system that helps one decode the meaning of Conscientização. The process involves he following questions that are addressed in a Conscientização dialogue:

Naming:

Examples of Naming Questions:

What are the most dehumanizing problems in "Dwight's" life?
Should things be as they are?
How should they be?

Reflecting:

Examples of Reflecting Questions:

Why are things this way?
Who is to blame?
What is your role in the situation?

Acting:

Examples of Acting Questions:

What can be done?
What should be done?
What have you done or will you do?

The analysis of data collected by administering these questions was factor analyzed in Smith's dissertation and established decoding constructs or themes based on the level of consciousness. The most critical conscious level that shows deconstruction of internalized oppression that liberates one from the oppressor is referred to as a *"Critical Conscious Level"* that leads to taking appropriate action as a liberated thinker whether you are uneducated or not. As illustrated in the next image that exhibits Conscientização in action (extracted from: Smith, 1975, "Conscientização": An Operational Definition. University of Massachusetts Amherst (Dissertation).

```
            d.   Generalizes from one oppressive system to
                 another
   C.   Acting

        1.   Self-Actualizing
             a.   Seeks appropriate role models
             b.   Personal/ethnic self-esteem
             c.   Self-growth/transforming learning
             d.   Subject/actor
             e.   Faith in peers/peer learning
             f.   Boldness/risk-taking/unorthodox solutions
             g.   Reliance on community resources/participation
             h.   Opposes oppressor groups

        2.   Transforming the System
             a.   Dialogue-polemics
             b.   Comradeship
             c.   Scientific approach
             d.   Change norms/laws/procedures

   SUMMARY

        Conscientizacao is a process of growth through three distinct
   but interrelated stages: magical, naive, and critical consciousness.
   Archetypical  magical  individuals  conform  to  the  oppressive
   situation in which they find themselves.

                                                              6
```

Freire's methods opened my insights on correcting the wrongs in the way we view African heritage from a liberated mindset that is described well by another Freire scholar, Jane Vella (2018) who coded learning as a Dialogue by conceptualizing Freire's coding methods of consciousness. Vella states the following:

**"The Means is Dialogue, and the End of Dialogue is Learning, and the Purpose of Learning is Peace (Vella, 2018)."**

This consciousness-approach led me to start viewing African identity from an African centered view and helped me decode the meaning of _"internalized oppression"_ and how to respond to the attitudes that cause oppression. This then thereby led to how to unpack the impact and the effects of _"internalized oppression"_ without blaming myself or others. The 21st Century and the 2020 world-wide pandemic has revealed just how much how the _**"African Diaspora"**_ has transformed the world and why it is also going to be the solution to the world in terms of peace. As long as we take time to carefully, precisely, and critically unpack and decode the causes and effects of all forms of **oppression** and its infamous antecedent **suppression** by becoming conscious of the impact that the **African Diaspora** has had as a heritage we can more proactively forward. Recognizing the effects and affects that the **African Diaspora** has built on the global world and now how it is the positive solution to the worlds conflicts towards _**peace**_.

An In-Depth and Detailed Summary of the African Heritage in America that has become the African Diaspora

When Europeans brought slaves out of Africa, they brought men and women who were a part of a well-organized family and kinship system that had held together for centuries. The legitimization of marriage in Africa was no less formal, durable, or important than in Europe. This system was unknown to Europeans who, out of ignorance, concluded that Africans had not developed a culture.

This attitude took a long time to change. Even those who eventually learned that there was an African civilization before European conquest, still assumed that African cultures were too shallow to survive slavery. Even among educated Americans, Black and White alike, some inaccurately believe and still perpetuate the erroneous belief that somehow *"slavery destroyed the Black family."* Undoubtedly, decades of one-sided education, biased toward Anglo-centered views of history, have created the image of helpless blacks waiting for someone to free them so that the "white man" can give them a lick of Western Education (Reid, Lee, Jedlicka, Shin, 1977).

Slavery did not destroy the black family, because black couples were willing to die, rebel, or escape from their masters to keep their families intact. The threat of escape and a willingness to die for their principles kept most slave owners from interfering in their slaves' family lives. Margaret Garner is an example of how black determination kept the owners from interfering with the black family unity:

"Each year in the antebellum era, approximately a thousand slaves fled northward to escape bondage. Most walked on foot, traveling at night, and slept in barns and woods. Margaret Garner, a fugitive slave, killed two of her children rather than permit them to be returned to slavery. After her capture by slave catchers, she drowned herself in the Ohio River (Mintz & Kellogg, 1988, caption to a picture. "Slave Mother." (Between pages 92 and 93)"

Population geneticists in the 20th century corroborate Douglass' observation (Mazur & Robertson, 1972). They describe the American-Black as an emergent population with genetic characteristics of the Western and Northern European, American Indian, Forest African, and Bantu among others (Mazur & Robertson, 1972, p. 69). Of course, what makes the American-Black an important culture in American history is not their biological makeup but their cultural heritage and their continual, perpetual, and innovative role in the ongoing development of an open, inventive, and socially-conscious democratic society in America.

Then the question may be asked: why then refer to Black United States citizens as American-Black and not Black-American? A good question. Once during a late-night radio talk show, a black male called in and said to the talk show host: "You've been saying "Afro-American."—I am not an African, I am American and I am Black. I am an American-Black." He went on to explain how putting "American" first was symbolic to him of what element of his identity comes from and what he most aspires and associates to.

The African heritage can be credited with this kind of determination that preserved large numbers of cohesive, black families. Slavery extinguished the rituals and customs of the African marriage and family life, but the strong kin ties learned in Africa were transferred from generation to generation. With time, owners and slaves learned to live by an unwritten code: owners would respect the slave family, and slaves would refrain from rebellion and escape.

The Civil War brought an end to slavery, but it also brought on new hardships. Not being beaten by slavery, American-Blacks now faced reconstruction and endured another phase of hardship: racial inequity, economic inequity, social inequity, outright bigotry, and systemic murder and violence. Which are the framework of "externalized oppression" leading to "internalized oppression" and are the quintessential essence of this narrative and its focus on the problems with HBCU Culture. This establishes the need for Conscientização and its ability to aid in *"Identity Reconstruction"*.

A *concept* is an abstract idea that cannot be observed directly. The word *"race"* qualifies as a concept because one has to have an observable definition of that concept for the word to be applicable in daily life. The definition that allows the observation of a concept is called an *"operational definition"*. Operational definitions of race vary over time and across ethnic groups. In his study of the etymology of the word *"race"*, Smedly (1998) found that different European cultures developed different meanings of the concept *"race"*. The Portuguese and Spanish constructed a continuous flow of observable biological traits among people, so that they did not construct a rigid set of racial categories. For example, they perceived the skin color in various shades of white and black. Combinations of black and white were recognized without rigid boundaries. The Anglo-Saxon construction of race in Australia, South Africa, and in Anglo-America relied on boundaries based on person's skin color. A person could be either white or one of the arbitrary non-white categories. One such racially based ethnic group is the American-Black. Smedley (1998) states the following:

"Beliefs about one's own physical traits or race can be the basis for the formation of ethnic groups. "Race" as an element of ethnic identity without an associated belief, is no more than a socially constructed, ethnic category. One's awareness of being categorized, however, is enough for a person to have a sense of ethnic identity based on race. Beliefs about the virtues, history or migration of a race, according to Weber, facilitate ethnic group formation (p. 289)."

The usual definition of *ethnic identity* refers to the "individual's sense of belonging to an ethnic group and the degree to which his or her thinking, feeling, and behavior is due to ethnic-group's membership" (Rotheram-Borus et al, 1998). According to the original work on ethnic identity published in Germany by Max Weber (1910) in the early part of the twentieth century, an individual can have an ethnic identity without a sense of membership to an ethnic group. Roth and Wittich (1968) translated Weber's study to mean that ethnic membership does not necessarily constitute a group: *"it only facilitates group formation of any kind, particularly in the political sphere"* (p. 389). In other words, an individual's awareness of one's own beliefs, race, and national or regional origin are enough to form an ethnic identity even if an individual does not have a sense of belonging to an organized ethnic group. Only through addressing negative attitudes and perceptions towards ideas about race, ethnic identity, and issues that internally inhibit self-growth can marginalization and all forms of oppression be addressed from an individualistic standpoint for the betterment and holistic healing of all. The African Diaspora is unique in that it addresses the seminal issues in the aforesaid and creates a unique opportunity for collaboration, unity, and healing. Once issues pertaining towards differences, misunderstandings, and past offenses are openly discussed and addressed via the "Conscientização Process" then more opportunities for partnership and universal projects can be explored and put into action. These are the first steps towards healing on a global scale and the operationalization of *"Cracking the HBCU Culture Code"*.

A Final "Cracking the HBCU Culture Code" Book Summary

After more than 50 years Paulo Freire's *"Pedagogy of the Oppressed"* still rings true. Now more than ever it is time that we put into action his methods such as: *"Conscientização"* to heal from a global pandemic and its physical, social, and emotional aftermath. Freire's methods can go along way in aiding us to *"Crack the HBCU Culture Code"* and liberate the masses from the ongoing ramifications of *"internalized oppression"*. The methodology is sound and has been extensively put into practice. It is both of the author's hopes that "Conscientização" along with the many other solutions provided within the confines of this text are used to address all of the aforementioned problems that were identified therein. Hopefully and prayerfully the abovementioned answers provided in all of the previous chapters will be actively put into practice to uplift, heal, and educate. Thus, we safeguard the future by ensuring that HBCUs will not only continue to exist, but also thrive on their respective campuses. Thereby continuing to uphold each of their core missions that are inherent in the education, production and service, and graduation of future generations of problem-solvers, innovators, and scholars who impact and change the world for the continual benefit of all.

References

Banks, J.A. (1993). Multicultural Education for Young Children: Racial and Ethnic Attitudes and their Modification. In B. Spodek (Ed.), Handbook of research on the education of young children (pp), 236-250). New York: Macmillan.

Banks, J.A. (2001). Cultural diversity and education: Foundations, curriculum, and, teaching. (4th Ed.). Boston: Allyn and Bacon.

Belenky, M.F. , Clinchy, B.M., Goldberger, N.R. & Tarule. J.M. (1997). Women's ways of knowing: The Development of Self, Voice, and Mind. New York: Basic Books.

Brown, C. (1978). Literacy in 30 Hours: Paulo Freire's Process in Northeast Brazil. Alternative Schools Network.

Carter, N. (2003). Convergence or divergence: Alignment of standards, assessment, and issues of diversity. AACTE. Washington, DC.

Carnoy, M. (1975). Education as cultural imperialism: A reply. *Comparative Education Review*, *19*(2), 286-289.

Delpit, L. (1995). Other people's children: Cultural conflict in the classroom. New York: The New Press.

Espinoza-Herold, M. (2003).Issues in Latino Education: Race, School Culture, and Politics of Academic Success. Boston: Pearson education Group, Inc.

Gay, G. (2000). Culturally responsive teaching: Theory, research, and practice. New York: Teachers College Press.

Illich, I., Illich, I., Illich, I., & Illich, I. (1971). Deschooling Society.

Irvine, J.J. (2003). Educating teachers for diversity: Seeing with a cultural eye. Teacher College Press. New York, NY.

Kohl, A. (1994). "I won't Learn from You": and Other Thoughts on Creative Maladjustment. New York: New York Press.

Landsman, J., & Lewis, C.W. (2006). White teachers/diverse classrooms: A guide to building inclusive schools, promoting high expectations, and eliminating racism. Stylus. Sterling, VA.

Lyotard, J. (1984). The postmodern condition: A report on knowledge. Minneapolis: University of Minnesota Press.

McLaren, P. (1998). Life in schools: An introduction to critical pedagogy in the foundations of education. (3rd Ed.). New York: Longman.

Mintz, S., & Kellogg, S. (1989). Domestic revolutions: A social history of American family life. Simon and Schuster.

Perry, T., Steele, C., & Hilliard, A. (2003). Young, gifted, and black: Promoting high achievement among African American students. Beacon Press. Boston, MA.

Reid, J. D., Lee, E. S., Jedlicka, D., & Shin, Y. (1977). Trends in black health. Phylon (1960-), 38(2), 105-116.

Rotheram-Borus, M. J., Lightfoot, M., Moraes, A., Dopkins, S., & LaCour, J. (1998). Developmental, ethnic, and gender differences in ethnic identity among adolescents. Journal of Adolescent Research, 13(4), 487-507.

Smedley, A. (1998). " Race" and the construction of human identity. *American anthropologist*, *100*(3), 690-702.

Smith, W. A. (1975). "Conscientização": An Operational Definition. University of Massachusetts Amherst (Dissertation).

Tatum, B. D. (2017). *Why are all the Black kids sitting together in the cafeteria?: And other conversations about race.* Hachette UK.

Thomas-Robinson, M., Hopson, R., & Sengupta, S. (2004). In search of cultural competence in evaluation: Toward principles and practices. *New Directions for Evaluation. 102, Summer.*

Villegas, A.M., & Lucas, T. (2002). Educating culturally responsive teachers: A coherent approach. Suny Press. Albany, NY.

Vella J. (2018). *The little blue book of dialogue education: The essentials.* Lambert Academic Publishing.

Weber, M. (1910). Max Weber on race and society.

Weber, M. (1971). Max Weber on race and society (Trans.). Social Research, 38, 30-41. (Original work published 1910).

Wink, J. (2005). Critical pedagogy: Notes from the real world (p. 167). New York, NY: Pearson/Allyn & Bacon.

www.ingramcontent.com/pod-product-compliance
Lightning Source LLC
Chambersburg PA
CBHW050416110426
42812CB00006BA/1908